IS THERE A RETIREMENT CRISIS?

An Exploration of the Current Debate

George A. (Sandy) Mackenzie

Statement of Purpose

The CFA Institute Research Foundation is a not-for-profit organization established to promote the development and dissemination of relevant research for investment practitioners worldwide.

Cover photo credit: Julien Fourniol/Baloulumix / Moment / Getty Images

ISBN: 978-1-952927-00-3

Biography

George A. (Sandy) Mackenzie, a native of Nova Scotia, came to the United States over 40 years ago to take up a position on the economic staff of the International Monetary Fund, where he worked for over 25 years. In the latter part of his Fund career, among other assignments he led technical assistance missions to countries in Central America, Central Europe, the Middle East and francophone Africa on a variety of public financial issues, including public pension reform and social expenditure issues. He and his staff also prepared papers for the Fund's executive board on pension and other public policy issues. After leaving the Fund, Mr. Mackenzie joined the staff of AARP's Public Policy Institute as their pensions expert. Following his stint with AARP, he became the inaugural editor of the *Journal of Retirement*, which publishes papers by both academics and practitioners on the economic and financial aspects of retirement, and oversaw the first five years of the JOR's existence. He now writes occasionally on a broad range of retirement-related issues.

Sandy Mackenzie is the author of two books: *Annuity Markets and Pension Reform* (2006), and *The Decline of the Traditional Pension* (2010), both published by Cambridge University Press. He has also authored or co-authored articles on public financial issues for various academic journals, as well as many papers on pension and retirement security issues for various publishers. *Is There a Retirement Crisis?* is his most recent major work.

Sandy lives in Washington D.C. with his wife, Carolyn, and their daughter Marjorie. He is an enthusiastic amateur musician, singing in his church choir, and playing the piano. He also plans to return to the five-string banjo, which he took up as a child. The study of Biblical Hebrew rounds off his leisurely pastimes.

Contents

PL Qualified Activity CFA Institute This publication qualifies for 4 PL credits under the guidelines of the CFA Institute Professional Learning Program.

Acknowledgements

To my Macdonald Cousins: Margaret, Isabel, and Donald.

The author is indebted to participants at a Pew Research Center seminar held in September 2017 and to participants at a seminar sponsored by the Tax Economists' Forum held at the Tax Foundation in September 2019. He also thanks Lori Lucas, Jack VanDerhei, Craig Copeland, John Mueller, Meir Statman, Anna Rappaport, Marjorie Mackenzie, and especially Larry Siegel for their comments and drafting suggestions. However, he is solely responsible for any errors of fact or interpretation in this study.

1. Introduction

The current debate over the retirement prospects of workers worldwide has attracted the attention of many distinguished economists. Like other policy debates, it has resulted in a marked divergence if not a polarization of views, even if the debate has remained civil. Those researchers who believe a crisis exists—the crisis advocates—have concluded, in some cases, that, by the yardstick they use, more than half the population of the United States (the country for which data are most readily obtained) is at risk for material hardship as they age. One researcher has concluded that 90% of working Americans may be at risk.

The more skeptical students of the US situation—the retirement crisis skeptics—take an opposite view. These researchers tend to concede that some portion, perhaps a significant share, of the population is either not prepared or not preparing adequately for retirement. But they do not view a generalized policy change, such as an increase in Social Security benefits, as the right solution. They do not discern a general crisis.

This monograph is motivated by a concern for retirement worldwide. Given the size and scope of the problem, however, we have limited our coverage to the G–7 group of major industrial countries plus Australia. Because such a large share of the detailed research pertains to the United States, Chapters 2 and 3 deal exclusively with that country. Chapter 4 offers an overall assessment of that research, and Chapter 5 presents a cross-country study of both pension and health issues that compares the institutional and macrofeatures of the United States with those of the other seven countries.

Some observers would ascribe the considerable differences in the outlook of researchers this work analyzes to political bias. Conservatives tend to be more optimistic about the financial preparedness of retirees and would-be retirees than liberals. A basic reason for the difference, however, is the sheer difficulty of forming a reliable view of the nature of the problem. It is much harder to be definite about the preparedness for retirement of young and middle-age workers than it is for those nearing retirement or those who already have retired.

Nonetheless, even hazarding a view about the prospects of those Americans who already have retired is no small task. Forecasting the future financial condition of a household is extremely difficult, particularly when that future is 20 to 30 years away. Even for older households, planning for retirement is fraught with difficulty. We do not know how long we will live, or what the future state of our health will be. We continue to face investment and sequence-of-returns risks if we expect to extract equity from our home or intend to rely to some extent in retirement on income from financial assets. The formal insurance mechanisms that are available to hedge these risks are imperfect and are hard for most people to understand. It is not surprising under the circumstances that even experts disagree. An additional source of difficulty is differences in the choice of yardstick to measure financial sustainability in retirement.

This monograph attempts to narrow, even if it cannot entirely eliminate, the differences between the opposing camps. The process begins with a survey of the conceptual issues that arise in assessing retirement preparedness: the significance and usefulness of measures of the replacement ratio and related issues, such as the impact of changing household composition as its members age and the appropriate treatment of housing equity. It then turns to analyzing the major risks that aging households face: health care and long-term care cost uncertainties, investment and sequence-of-returns risk, longevity risk, and political risk. This analysis places its emphasis on institutions rather than on quantitative analysis.

This discussion of basic issues sets the stage for our review of the work of the two sides presented in Chapter 3. That review begins with a detailed analysis of the work of prominent crisis advocates and continues with the retirement crisis skeptics. Chapter 3 is somewhat technical, but its basic arguments can be understood without a sophisticated grasp of the technical details. The chapter closes with a brief discussion of the findings of four retirement confidence surveys conducted by well-known institutions, getting the answers from the horse's mouth, as it were.

Following an assessment of US studies in Chapter 4, Chapter 5 then reviews and compares the major structural features of the pension and health care systems of the major industrial countries—the United States and the other six countries that make up the G–7, plus Australia. It does not duplicate the analysis of Chapters 2 and 3 for this group of countries, but by comparing the structural features of these countries, it aims to put in relief some of the study's assessments of the US situation and thus makes the study international in its scope.

2. Conceptual Difficulties and Special Risks with Assessments of Retirement Security

Conceptual Difficulties

Any assessment of the likelihood of a particular household or age cohort enjoying a financially secure retirement must address several complicated and intricate issues. The most basic issues are longevity risk, health risk, investment risk, and political risk. But, to these, one must add the issue of the replacement rate, a concept that must be defined before that rate can be determined for a given investor. The basic definition of the replacement rate is the ratio of projected income in retirement to a measure of working income, which is often average income in the last five or so years before retirement. The concept can be tricky to grasp, as we discuss next, because it can be defined and used in different ways.

Other issues include the following:

- The implication of changes in household size as retirement approaches (these changes have implications for the calculation of the replacement rate);
- The role of nonrecurring expenditure in determining the adequacy of the standard replacement ratio that a household either expects to achieve or has chosen as a target;
- The appropriate treatment of housing equity;
- The appropriate assumption for the pattern of household expenditure in retirement, given the tendency for households, as they age, to reduce expenditure on more physically demanding activities and pastimes, and to increase their health-related expenditure; and
- The possibility that the increasing likelihood of death as a household ages may cause some frontloading of expenditure.

Another issue is the time period used to measure the average or typical level of working income.

The Replacement Rate and Its Interpretation. The replacement rate is a basic tool employed by financial advisers who deal with retirement preparation. It can be either descriptive, a measurement of what is or what is expected to be, or it can be normative, that is, a goal or target. As an example of the descriptive use of the term, consider an old-fashioned defined benefit (DB) pension plan that pays a pension equal to 40% of the final salary of a plan member. In this case, we may say that the plan has a replacement rate of 40%.

When retirement planners are advising clients who are preparing for retirement, they typically are talking about a target—that is, an objective that they would like to have their clients achieve. For a variety of well-known reasons, including the reduced need to save for retirement once retirement begins, the cessation of work-related expenditures, and the favorable tax treatment of postretirement income compared with working income, sustaining the same standard of living in retirement as that which we experienced while working does not require as high an income.

Hence, the targeted replacement rate is always less than one. The fraction of income that needs to be replaced in retirement to maintain the standard of living can, in principle, be calculated given the parameters of the tax system and knowledge of a household's saving propensities and work-related expenditure. An additional adjustment can, or could ideally, be made for nonrecurring expenditures that end around the time retirement starts: mortgage payments (if the mortgage is close to being paid off), tuition payments for student household members, and commuting costs.

It is common for advisers to set a replacement rate target in the neighborhood of 70% to 75%, on the assumption that the standard of living obtained while working can be maintained at that ratio. It should be emphasized, however, that a marked change in a household's economic prospects as it nears retirement, or simply a lack of good planning can render a given target for the replacement rate completely unfeasible. As an example, suppose that a household had an annual income during working life of $100,000, and had managed to accumulate financial wealth of $1,000,000. It had planned to withdraw $35,000 each year in interest, dividends, and capital gains plus a modest encroachment on capital, which together with Social Security benefits of $35,000, would maintain its preretirement standard of living more or less indefinitely. A drop in the market of 50% would reduce its feasible withdrawal to $17,500. If the crash occurs within five years from the state of planned retirement, maintaining the 70% replacement rate target would require that most of the household's preretirement income would have to be devoted to savings to reconstitute its financial assets. Faced with the choice of such severe austerity, the typical and presumably sensible household would abandon its 70% replacement target, which would no longer be optimal.

Defining and Measuring the Denominator of the Replacement Rate. Assuming that it is feasible for a household to aim for a standard of living in retirement that approximates the standard of living it achieved during working life, how should the standard of living during working life be measured? In principle, some measure of personal expenditure (consumption) during working life should be the basis for the calculation. The basic goal of retirement planning then would be to adjust saving and investment policy as necessary so that consumption during retirement would not be substantially different from what it was while the retiree was working.

In practice, financial planners rely on measures of income, not consumption. It is assumed that consumption in retirement will be equal to consumption during working life if income in retirement equals (or exceeds) the targeted replacement rate times income during working life. This is not always a good assumption, because changes in consumption can differ from changes in income (whether that is pre- or postretirement income) in either direction and for varied reasons. It's consumption that matters.

The standard approach is to take an average of working income over a period of several years that ends at retirement. In addition to the fact that, in some circumstances, the standard replacement rate may not be a practical target, the question arises of how many years of working-life income should be averaged. Social Security includes a worker's 35 best earning years in calculating its retirement benefit: retirement planners typically take a much shorter period at the end of their client's career, perhaps 5 years.

How long the period should be depends on a household's perception of its customary income level. If a household's income has risen strongly and is much higher at career's end than it was over most of the career, averaging income over a very long period does not make a lot of sense. If the household has quickly gotten used to a high income level, it may want to maintain that income level and the standard of living that income level pays for in retirement. In this case, applying a conventionally calculated replacement rate (i.e., in the range of 70–80%) to career average income will result in a target for income in retirement that is far too low.[1]

Of course, someone who had experienced a rapid increase in income at career's end may not have saved enough to maintain this end-of-career living standard; the earner simply will have to scale back expenses in retirement.

[1]For example, if the replacement ratio calculated using an average of income over a 35-year career is 70%, assuming growth in income is a constant 2% per year, it drops to 53% when income is averaged over the past five years of work. The more rapid is income growth, the greater the difference between the replacement rates calculated in these two different wage growth scenarios.

If, instead, income had fluctuated over an extended period without showing an obvious trend, averaging income over a longer period would make more sense. In this case, the replacement rates calculated using a career average and an end-of-career average would be closer to one another.

The lesson to be drawn from these examples is that the period over which income is to be averaged to calculate the denominator of the replacement rate is to some extent arbitrary, or at least that it is a matter of personal preference. A related point in calculating the replacement rate is to recognize that, for income in retirement to provide the same standard of living as the years pass, it must rise with inflation. That is, it must be indexed to some indicator of aggregate consumer prices. If income from a pension is fixed in nominal terms, it has to be converted to a flow of indexed income, which will reduce the measured replacement rate.[2]

Financial planners have recognized for some time that not all working-life income has to be replaced, as we have seen. More recently, however, a number of economists have argued that the conventional adjustments for saving, work-related expenditure, and a change in the tax regime do not go far enough (Kotlikoff 2007).[3] Among other criticisms, they maintain that a series of nonrecurring expenditures like mortgage payments and tuition, if they are coming to an end, should be dropped from the measure of working income. These economists contend that the part of the income of a working household that is covering these expenditures need not be replaced in retirement. In addition, the part of working income devoted to saving for retirement also should be dropped; again, it is consumption that matters.

Table 1 presents an illustrative example of how ignoring temporary or nonrecurring expenditures can result in a misleading estimate of the replacement rate. The table depicts a simplified household income statement, expressed in real terms, for a household as it approaches retirement, and then in the first few years of retirement. Gross income falls from $75,000 at the end of working life to $45,000 as retirement begins, because the sum of income from investments (unearned income), Social Security, and pensions cannot compensate fully for the elimination of earned income. Other expenditures, however, notably mortgage repayments and tuition, are phased out (although a few families approaching retirement still may be struggling with student debt), and the tax burden declines, reflecting the favorable taxation

[2]Brady (2010) makes this point.

[3]ES Planner, the retirement planning software used by the company that Professor Laurence Kotlikoff founded, is based on an optimization approach, and takes account of nonrecurring expenditure.

Table 1. An Illustration of the Unreliability of the Conventionally Calculated Replacement Rate (income and expenditure in inflation-adjusted dollars)

	Last Years of Work (annual averages)	Annual Income in Retirement
Income		
Earned income	70,000	
Unearned income	5,000	5,000
Social Security	—	27,000
Employer-provided pension	—	13,000
Gross income	75,000	45,000
Taxes	15,000	6,500
After-tax income	60,000	38,500
Expenditure		
College and other temporary expenditure	19,000	—
Mortgage interest	500	—
Mortgage principal	2,000	—
Regular household expenditure	38,500	38,500
Saving (ex. mortgage payment and temporary exp.)	—	—
Conventionally calculated replacement rate (in percent)		60.0

Source: Author's calculations.

of Social Security and the progressivity of the combined federal and state income tax system.

This example has been constructed so that recurrent household expenditure does not fall in retirement. The household's financial assets are not eroded, and they continue to generate the same modest amount of income as they did previously. Although the household is able to maintain its expenditure level, the replacement rate as conventionally measured is only 60%, a rate that most financial planners would reject as inadequate. Note that if the stock of wealth at the beginning of retirement were much less than the level assumed in Table 1, the preretirement household expenditure level could not be sustained postretirement. The stock of wealth would fall, and unearned income would drop off.

Wage Versus Price Indexation. In addition to the issue of how long a period should be used to derive the working-life income average (i.e., the denominator of the replacement rate), a debate continues over which inflation rate to use for converting wages and salaries to current dollars. As Biggs (2017) argues, indexation according to the consumer price index (CPI) is consistent with the standard version of the life-cycle theory, which maintains that the purchasing power of income should count and be smoothed over time.

Wage indexation is the adjustment of past income based on the growth rate of wages since the date in the past when the wage was earned. For example, if average wages have increased by 10% in the past five years, then a salary of $30,000 earned five years ago should be increased to $33,000 to determine the measure of working-life income used to calculate the replacement rate. By making this adjustment, wage indexation assumes that workers should partake in the increase in productivity—the whole increase—because they earned the salary. Put another way, the basic assumption justifying wage indexation is that retiring workers deserve a standard of living that reflects the standard of living of current workers.[4]

Because wages normally grow faster than prices, a retirement income that simply maintains the retired worker's standard of living will fall short of the income needed to keep pace with the income of current workers. If, however, our concern is maintaining the standard of living in retirement, and not the relative position of retired workers vis-à-vis current workers, indexation to consumer prices rather than wage indexation should be preferred.

Implications of a Change in the Composition of a Household. When children leave home and become financially independent, the household's expenditures typically decline without lowering the parents' standard of living. Economists have formulated equivalence scales, which can be used to estimate how the presence of children can affect the size of a family's budget needed to maintain the parents' standard of living. One such scale is given by the following formula, where E stands for adult equivalence, A is the number of adults, and C is the number of children.

$$E = (A + 0.7 \times C)^{0.7}.$$

The adult equivalence of a household with two adults and two children is 2.4 (about two and a half adults) and that for a household with a childless couple is 1.6, reflecting the economies of scale from cohabitation in addition to the absence of children. These numbers imply that the addition of two children to a previously childless household would require an increase in

[4]The Social Security Administration (SSA) calculates retirement benefits using wage indexation to adjust past wages to current dollars, but then uses the Consumer Price Index (CPI) to provide cost-of-living adjustments once the worker has retired.

the household budget of about 50% to maintain the standard of living. (This ignores any decrease in parental income resulting from having the children.)

Consequently, when the children leave home, the budget could shrink, in principle, by about a third without affecting the couple's standard of living. Suppose that this phenomenon had been ignored when the couple planned their retirement, having set a target replacement rate of 70%. The target replacement rate could decline to 47% (of the income needed when children were in the household) without lowering the couple's standard of living. If the family had only one child, the replacement rate could still drop to about 60%.

These simple examples illustrate the potential of family downsizing for improving a couple's standard of living, and for reducing the resources needed to sustain the standard of living in retirement. This reduction does require, however, that the parents realize that a decline in total household expenditure does not have to imply a decline in their well-being.

Studies of this issue have not been conclusive. Coe and Webb (2010) find that household expenditure does not change when its size declines. Their study has been criticized by Pang and Schieber (2014) for being based on too small a sample size. A more recent study by Dushi, Munnell, Sanzenbacher, and Webb (2016) finds only a small negative effect. Other studies have found that household composition does have an effect on expenditure. In particular, Scholz and Seshadri (2009) found that households in the second-lowest quartile of the distribution of lifetime income with three children had a net worth that was 15% lower than that of childless households. Presumably, once the children have flown the nest, the household that had children would be able to build up its net worth and also increase its personal expenditure.

Even if a household wishes to keep its expenditure level unchanged after the children leave, it does not follow that any decline in expenditure would necessarily entail a decline in the standard of living of its remaining members. That said, the increase in spending per remaining member of the household might be seen as a reward for the long years of childrearing and the deferral of expenditure to finance their upbringing and education. In these circumstances, a couple whose children have left home might feel resentful if the income freed up by the ending of childcare responsibilities were not theirs to spend while the parents are still relatively young. Thus, the issue remains unresolved.

The Trend and Composition of Expenditure in Retirement. The standard replacement rate calculation usually assumes that a household's targeted expenditure in real terms during retirement does not change. In fact, the evidence suggests that both the level and the composition of expenditure do change during retirement. In particular, health care expenditure increases, whereas work-related expenditure tends to decline fairly drastically at the beginning of retirement (Banerjee 2015). These changes in expenditure composition, having no effect on the *level* of expenditure, do not have to affect a household's targeted replacement rate during retirement; however, targeted replacement rates should consider any trend involving a decline or increase in total expenditure.

The composition of expenditure aside, some evidence suggests that total expenditure tends to decline in retirement. For example, Banerjee (2015) finds that average spending falls in the two initial postretirement years and continues to fall thereafter. Butrica, Goldwyn, and Johnson (2005) also find that median expenditure drops from age 53–64 to age 65–74 and drops again from that age bracket to age 75 and older. Part of this decrease could reflect retrenchment made necessary by poorer-than-expected investment performance, unexpected health expenditures, or a more basic lack of planning. It is also possible that households "frontload" their expenditure to some degree, because increasing mortality reduces the likelihood that a household's members will be around in future years, causing them to discount future consumption.[5]

This last assumption underlies the approach of economists who have addressed the difficult issue of whether households have saved optimally for retirement, which we discuss in Chapter 3. Advancing years and the advent and accumulation of physical and mental infirmities might reduce expenditure on activities requiring robust health, including travel far from home and trusted medical care facilities.

Even a small decline in expenditure, if it persists, can substantially reduce total expenditure in retirement. Over a period of 30 years, for example, and assuming a discount rate of 3% per annum, an annual decrease of 1.5%—for example, for every $10,000 spent last year, only $9,850 is spent this year—will reduce total expenditure over the period by 21%. If the optimum replacement rate had been calculated to be 75% on the assumption of unchanged expenditure, the true replacement rate would be closer to 60%. By comparison, a drop in expenditure of 10% (in total, not per year) over the first five years of retirement, but with a full recovery after that, has a relatively modest impact on the present discounted value of total expenditure.

[5]Standard neoclassical optimization theory assumes that an individual discounts the satisfaction expected from future consumption by the probability that the individual will still be alive to enjoy it. How much effect this discounting has on planned future consumption depends on how strongly households desire to smooth their consumption over time (see Milevsky 2011). There is an optionality consideration: if the person is alive at an advanced age, that person will need the money, making frontloading of expenditures less attractive.

Hurd and Rohwedder (2008), using data from the Health and Retirement Study (HRS), and the auxiliary Consumption and Activities Mail Survey, find that expenditure does tend to decline during retirement. They attribute most of that decline, however, to the combined effects of the following:

(1) substitution of home production for commercial preparation (e.g., home-prepared meals take the place of ready-to-eat meals, take-out, and dining out, time no longer being scarce);

(2) a decline in work-related expenditure (e.g., spending on commuting to and from work); and

(3) unexpected declines in wealth in the wake of unexpected job loss or illness.

The authors remark on the relative inertia of consumption, even in the face of large drops in income and wealth.[6]

The tendency for expenditure to decline during retirement has not been universally confirmed. Studies of the behavior of the expenditure of retired households have found considerable variations across households (Banerjee 2015). Expenditures by some households have tended to increase during retirement, perhaps because their initial assumptions about the financial outlook were too conservative. The studies that will be reviewed in Chapter 3 typically assume that postretirement expenditure is a constant. Given the evidence on expenditure trends, this is a defensible assumption to make, although the issue requires more investigation. If the tendency to substitute leisure time for expenditure is sufficiently strong, the replacement rate targeted for a household could be adjusted downward somewhat, however.

The Treatment of Home Equity. The equity in a retired household's home is an asset just like a 401(k) plan or a bank account. Economists treat an owner-occupier as a landlord who rents to self and earns income in kind from that activity. Being an owner-occupier should reduce the household's expenditures and rental payments in particular. A household that owns its dwelling place outright is clearly better off than a household in otherwise identical financial circumstances living in an identical dwelling that it does not own, because it does not have to pay cash rent.

The fact that a household owns the house in which it lives, however, does not mean it can use the equity for general consumption. Everybody must live somewhere, so the proceeds from the sale of an owned house must be used

[6]Hurd and Rohwedder's work is explored at greater length in Chapter 3.

(in part or in whole) to make rent payments on another accommodation. The full proceeds cannot be devoted to meeting general expenditure needs.

Households whose members are very old and who sell their homes, opting to become renters rather than owner-occupiers, will need to finance a shorter stream of rental payments (albeit a stream of uncertain duration) than younger households in the same position. To that extent, these households may be able to extract funds from the sale of a home and not need those funds to pay for rented housing.[7]

Downsizing or moving to a locality with substantially lower housing costs are two other ways of extracting funds from the equity in a home. The benefits of downsizing depend in part on the transactions and related costs associated with the sale of a property. A common rule of thumb assumes that these costs are about 10% of the gross value of a sale, so that the sale of a $400,000 mortgage-free home nets the sellers about $360,000. Downsizing to a $300,000 home thus increases financial assets by $60,000, not $100,000. Given the assumptions in footnote 7, this sum will generate a 15-year income stream of about $5,000 per year.

A reverse mortgage (RM) is a less traditional way for retirees to unlock at least part of the equity of their home. The lending institution offers the household either a line of credit (the typical choice) or what is known as a monthly tenure payment—effectively a life annuity if the homeowner dies while still an occupant—which continues until the homeowner's death or the sale of the mortgaged property. The homeowner makes no repayments until the contract is terminated by death or the sale of the property. Upon the death of the homeowner, the payments made by the lender—to which a stipulated rate of interest applies—become due, but they cannot exceed 95% of the net selling price of the home.

RMs are complex and controversial instruments (see **Box 1** for a more complete description), and the market for them remains small.[8] As of end-July 2017, only one million Home Equity Conversion Mortgages (HECMs), which are federally insured and account for nearly the entire market, had been

[7]As an example, suppose that a couple, both of whose members are 85 years old, sells its house for $500,000 net of selling costs. They rent accommodation for $30,000 per year. Assuming an investment return of 5%, the couple could put aside about $311,000 to pay the rent until they both reached the age of 100. Assuming that they would not live past the age of 100, they could extract about $189,000 in equity from the sale. That sum would generate a 15-year annual income stream of about $18,000. Repeating these calculations for a couple age 70, the amount of equity that can be extracted from the sale is reduced to about $39,000. The corresponding annual income stream is reduced to about $2,500.

[8]Giordano (2015) is an accessible general reference on RMs. For a broader discussion of their potential role in financial planning, see Davidson and Turner (2015).

made since federal fiscal year 1990. The current annual volume of lending is about 60,000 mortgages, which is very small in relation to the conventional mortgage market.[9] Nonetheless, taking out an RM can substantially increase an older person's income.

Box 1. Reverse Mortgages

A reverse mortgage (RM) is in principle the most efficient way of extracting equity from a home. It gets its name from the fact that the arrangement pays the homeowner, rather than the reverse, which requires payments (of interest and principal) from the owner. The payments made by the lender take one or more of three forms: monthly payments, a partial or lump-sum payment, or a line of credit. In the case of a line of credit, interest is charged only on the credit actually extended. Credit outstanding grows at the same rate as the rate of interest charged on drawdowns. Homeowners (or their estate) make no payments until they sell the home or die. They are, however, responsible for paying property taxes, insurance, and maintenance charges. Homeowners failing to make these payments may be subject to foreclosure, and such foreclosures have to some extent tarnished the image of the RM. Upon the death of a borrower or a move, the borrower is responsible for the accumulated debt on the home or 95% of its appraised value, whichever is less.

Monthly payments may be either term payments or tenure payments. Term payments, as their name suggests, are fixed for a specific term. Tenure payments are paid until the homeowner's death or the sale of the property, whichever comes first. In this respect, an RM with tenure payments bears some resemblance to a life annuity.

The share of the property value that may be borrowed depends on the age of the youngest borrower or the nonborrowing spouse and on the rate of interest. The older the borrowers—the minimum age being 62—the greater the amount that may be borrowed. Borrowers must meet the FHA's creditworthiness guidelines, and any outstanding balance on a conventional mortgage must first be paid off. The HECM program, which sets the rules for RMs, is designed so that most loan balances never exceed the value of the home, which reduces lenders' risk.

[9]The small size of the RM market has been blamed on a combination of consumer ignorance and mistrust, and a dysfunctional market that hobbles consumers trying to make an informed choice between lenders and products (Knowledge@Wharton 2015).

As an illustration, taking out an RM on a home worth $300,000 could generate a monthly life tenure payment for a 75-year-old of about $1,100, which is large enough to substantially boost the disposable incomes of many older Americans.[10]

Because of the complications entailed in considering home equity, some researchers have ignored it. VanDerhei and Copeland (2010) simulate the impact on households that are at risk for inadequate retirement income of (1) taking out an RM at retirement or (2) selling the property when all other resources are exhausted and then moving to rental accommodation. Neither action significantly affected outcomes. Warshawsky (2017) has conducted an empirical study of the potential role that RMs might play in retirement. He argues that RMs are unlikely to be popular with households with limited net housing equity. Given his assumptions regarding the cost of an RM and the limits on the size of a loan relative to the value of the house, he concludes that the extra income they would generate in many cases would have only a modest impact on household income.

Warshawsky also argues that households with substantial financial as well as real assets would be better off with a conventional life annuity than a life tenure payment from an RM. This raises the question of whether the lack of popularity of conventional annuities might be negatively affecting the market for the RM equivalent. The same factors that inhibit demand for insurance company annuities that Warshawsky has enumerated could help explain the anemic size of the RM market as well.

Special Risks Facing Older Americans

A Note on Investment and Sequence-of-Returns Risk. Investment risk is an issue both for preretirees who plan to accumulate a reasonably sized portfolio of financial assets before they retire, and for retirees who plan to derive a significant part of their income from those assets once they retire. It is not an issue, or not much of one, for retirees in the bottom quintile of wealth, for whom financial assets are a small or negligible part of their wealth—including the capitalized value of Social Security—at retirement (Gustman, Steinmeier, and Tabatabai 2010).

Investment risk arises because the rates of return on virtually all financial assets are unpredictable. The nominal yield on fixed-interest securities is predictable, but the yield that will be obtained when those securities are redeemed and reinvested is not. Even when such assets are held to maturity, the lack of predictability of price inflation makes their real yield unpredictable.

[10]Tom Davison helped the author with this calculation, which is purely illustrative.

Note that equity returns are *really* unpredictable, and many retirees rely on them for capital growth and income.

Investment risk has another aspect to it: sequence-of-returns risk. If two investment funds from which no withdrawals are made (e.g., certain kinds of endowment funds) have the same average (geometric) return over the same period, the increase in the value of the two funds does not depend on the sequence of returns: whether the fat years or the lean ones come first, the appreciation in the value of the two funds will be the same. This equivalence will not be the case, however, when regular withdrawals are made from the fund, as a retiree would be likely to do. In this case, the sustainability of a given withdrawal pattern—for example, 3.5% of outstanding capital each year—will depend on the *order* of returns, not just on the *average* return over the period. It is better if the good years, when returns are above average, come first to minimize the chances of premature exhaustion of the fund. Of course, the investor does not control that; hence, the description of sequence-of-returns as a *risk*.

Standard portfolio theory assumes that investors will choose a point on their efficient frontier, which depicts the tradeoff between risk and return. Recent developments in behavioral portfolio theory imply a more complicated process. In any case, how investors saving for retirement should deal with risk is disputed. Target-date funds (TDFs) automatically lower the equity share (and thus the risk) of a retiree's portfolio as the retiree ages. This automaticity has the virtue of dealing with the problem of inertia—the tendency for investors, left to their own devices, to fail to adjust the composition of their portfolios as time passes. A simple TDF, with only equities and bonds, might gradually lower the share of equities so that by the year in which the investor turns 65, it has reached 60%. TDFs, however, are not without criticism. One criticism is that the glide path is lowering the share of contributions devoted to equities when the contributions are largest, which is toward the end of working life (Arnott, Sherrerd, and Wu 2013). Another criticism, albeit from a different angle, is that the share of equities reached at retirement remains sufficiently high that a collapse of the stock market can inflict a painful loss, such as occurred during the Great Recession. That said, the gains in portfolio value from maintaining a greater exposure to equities during working life could soften the impact of a market decline from a peak that would not have been reached with a more conservative strategy.

Investment and sequence-of-returns risk can be reduced but not eliminated. A conservatively structured portfolio will reduce market crash risk as well as sequence-of-returns risk. A bond-laddering strategy (i.e., one designed so that the value of bonds maturing in a given year equals, or at least does not exceed, the expenditure the portfolio is intended to finance in that year) is another possibility. Ideally, the longest bond maturity should extend well past the expected longevity of the investor. If it does not, then interest rate or reinvestment risk—that is, having to reinvest bond proceeds at a lower-than-planned interest rate—is an issue.

Apart from investment risk and sequence-of-returns risk, note that the expected rates of return to both equities and bonds have declined in recent years. This development, if it is a permanent change in the investment landscape, may be predictable and therefore not be a form of risk, but it does have clear implications for investors saving for retirement. Ilmanen, Rauseo, and Truax (2016) address the consequences of declining rates of return by simulating an investment model with future returns on stocks and bonds that are significantly lower than their average over the past 7 to 10 years.

The results are striking. With a real rate of return of 6.5% on a portfolio composed of 60% equity and 40% bonds, the authors find that a saving rate of 6% is enough to achieve the assumed target replacement rate of 75%. With a real rate of return of 5.5%, the required saving rate increases to 8%, and with a real rate of return of 3.5%, the required saving rate is no less than 15%. As we discuss in Chapter 3, investment risk is handled in diverse ways by different analysts and researchers.

Longevity Risk. Almost all older Americans are at least partially hedged against longevity risk—the risk of running out of money because of an unexpectedly long life. Social Security pays an indexed life annuity, and in the case of poorer Americans, it amounts to a very large share of their total (annuitized and nonannuitized) wealth (Gustman, Steinmeier, and Tabatabai 2010).

Longevity risk should in principle be more hedgeable than other risks older Americans face. It is possible to buy either a nominal or an indexed life annuity from an insurance company, but the market for both of these instruments, and that for deferred annuities, remains quite small.[11] Economists generally assume that people are underannuitized, a state they usually blame on several cognitive errors, in which reasonable initiatives are subverted by behavioral biases, like overdiscounting the likelihood of future losses.

Cognitive errors are not the whole story, however. Annuitizing 100% of one's wealth is clearly not sensible, because liquid assets would not be available to defray unexpected expenses. Employer-provided DB pensions, for those Americans who have one, increase the share of annuitized wealth. Fears as to

[11]See Mackenzie (2019) for a discussion of the relative merits of buying a single-period immediate annuity (SPIA) or a differed income annuity (DIA).

the solvency or probity of insurance companies cannot be simply dismissed as irrational; the last thing one wants at age 97 is a letter from the annuity issuer's receiver saying that the company has gone bankrupt and payments will stop.[12]

Statman (2017) argues that annuitization (beyond that provided by Social Security) is not a solution to retirement insecurity for many people, whether they may be among (to use his nomenclature) the poor, the precarious middle, or the rich. As he puts it, "an annuity solution mocks the precarious middle (people who either have low incomes or spend excessively) and the poor, whose meager savings make buying an annuity impracticable or impossible" (Statman 2017, p. 248).[13] Even if annuitization is feasible financially, an aversion by older Americans to encroaching on capital (which annuitization certainly does) may dampen demand. What is known as the availability bias may have the same effect: specifically, people can more easily visualize a scenario of premature death—the proverbial fear of being hit by a bus shortly after signing the annuity contract—than one of unexpectedly long life (Statman 2017, p. 233).[14]

Whatever the reasons for the small market for annuities, older Americans have effectively chosen to rely partly on self-insurance against longevity risk. In principle, a retired person can calculate the withdrawal rate from accumulated savings that would be sustainable, given projected expenditure for a period that significantly exceeds life expectancy. For example, someone who had just retired at age 65 could determine that, under what seems to be conservative assumptions about financial market returns, a withdrawal rate of about 3% could be sustained for 25 years, until reaching 90. This strategy would entail the slow decapitalization of the initial stock of assets.

---

[12]State insurance guaranty funds mitigate this risk, especially for smaller annuities, but these funds might also go bankrupt if there is a widespread financial system failure.

[13]Gustman, Steinmeier, and Tabatabai (2010) estimate that early baby boomers, who were between the ages of 51 and 56 in 2004 and in the bottom wealth decile, had median total wealth in 1992 dollars of $28,800 in 2004, of which $27,200 was accounted for by the capitalized value of expected Social Security benefits. This leaves virtually nothing to invest in other assets, including the annuities offered by life insurance companies. Early boomers in the next lowest decile had total wealth of $81,200, of which $64,200 was in the form of Social Security, again leaving little to invest in other assets. If the poorest (bottom decile) older Americans could save somewhat more and use those savings to buy an annuity, their already high rate of annuitization would only increase further. More affluent households who are well prepared for retirement but without a DB pension plan, in principle, could devote a moderate fraction of their wealth to an annuity without risking a liquidity crisis. This practice, while seemingly sensible, is not common.

[14]Statman's views are discussed further in Chapter 3. The limited guarantee period that may apply to an annuity in the event of the annuitant's early death does not dispel the availability bias, although it might mitigate it.

Alternatively, rather than making a precise calculation of the sustainable withdrawal rate, the retiree might simply adopt a rule of withdrawing only the income from investments. This might not be optimal in the rational world of neoclassical economists, in which income and capital are fungible, but it would keep the retiree from encroaching on capital at an excessive rate. It also could result in a sizable bequest, even if that outcome were not intended. A similar rule for investors holding equities is to spend only the dividends a share pays, and not the capital gains. Older Americans tend to hold stocks with higher dividend yields (Statman 2017, p. 230). Following the "spend-only-dividends" rule increases their spending above what it would be if their portfolio were more concentrated in lower-yielding stocks or in an index fund.

Health (Excluding Long-Term Disability) Risk. The degree of financial exposure of older Americans to large unforeseen expenditure from ill health changes dramatically at age 65, when virtually everyone becomes eligible for Medicare coverage. Before that, exposure to health risks depends on whether a household had medical insurance through a current or former employer or had been able to obtain an individual policy from an insurance company that provides adequate protection. These days, retired former company employees who used to be covered by their employer's health plan typically are no longer covered. Medicare with a supplementary policy to fill in gaps in Medicare's coverage can be expensive, although much less expensive than the insurance required by a person who is not covered by Medicare.[15]

Medicare has four parts. Part A covers hospital stays and Part B covers the doctor and other health service provider fees. All Americans 65 years and older normally are covered by both Parts A and B. Part C, which is known as Medicare Advantage, provides coverage through health management organizations (HMOs) and several other vehicles, and can substitute for Medicare Parts A and B; it is favored by those seeking minimal out-of-pocket (OOP) expenses. Part D is a prescription drug program offered by private insurers through Medicare. Some costs are shared between the insurer and the participant (the "doughnut hole"), but catastrophic coverage provision takes effect when OOP drug costs exceed a predetermined limit that varies from year to year.[16] Once OOP expenditure reach the specified figure, only a copayment or coinsurance will apply.

[15]Medicaid is intended for the poor. Its coverage of LTC is described later in this chapter in the section entitled "Risks Associated with Long-Term Care".

[16]Every person who qualifies for Medicare is automatically enrolled in Part A. Enrollment in Part B is voluntary, although more than 90% of those covered by Part A are enrolled in both (Kaiser Family Foundation 2015). Enrollment in Parts C and D is also voluntary, although 72% of those covered by Part A are also covered by Part D.

Medicare Parts A and B provide basic protection against the financial consequences of unexpected illness. Compared with the typical employer-provided plan, Medicare's coverage leaves its beneficiaries exposed to potentially large losses. The first night of a hospital stay of any length costs the participant $1,316 (although nights 2 through 60 are free), which means that someone who requires repeated hospitalizations can incur substantial costs. The copay for physicians' fees is 20%, and no stop-loss provision exists. As a result, a series of costly operations, procedures, or treatments could impose a heavy financial burden on the patient without a supplementary policy. Medicare Part D does put a cap on total copays for pharmaceuticals, but the cap is high enough that someone who requires expensive drugs could struggle with a heavy financial burden. Some older people also may find themselves requiring expensive or experimental drugs for the treatment of illnesses that their policy does not cover and that can cost hundreds of thousands of dollars.

Medicare is financed by government-set premiums and is adjusted periodically to reflect changes in program costs. Most participants in Part A do not pay a premium. Premiums for Part B are income related. As of 2020, these premiums begin at $144.60 per month. Beginning at $87,000 for a single person and $174,000 for a married couple filing jointly, premiums rise with income, reaching a maximum of $491.60 at an income of $500,000 for a single person and $750,000 for a couple. Part C premiums generally are set to equal Part B premiums, but participants in Part C may pay an additional premium for their plan. Part D premiums, like Part B premiums, are income related.

The gaps in Medicare's coverage explain why most Medicare beneficiaries have supplemented it with additional coverage. These additional policies include Medigap (supplementary insurance provided by private insurers according to specifications set by the government), employer-sponsored coverage (sometimes combined with Medigap), Medicare Advantage (sometimes combined with employer-sponsored insurance), Medicaid Advantage combined with Medicaid, and Medicaid only. In 2010, some 14% of Medicare beneficiaries had no additional coverage, and 6% were covered in other ways.

Medicaid provides additional coverage for older Americans who are eligible for both Medicare and Medicaid (so-called dual eligibles) by helping to pay for premiums or OOP costs. Medicare Advantage, which replaces Medicare Parts A and B, provides additional protection through a stop-loss provision.

In sum, one in seven Medicare beneficiaries lacks the protection of a supplementary policy. Beneficiaries who do have this protection do not face the prospect of a catastrophic loss, but serious or chronic illness still could entail expenditures high enough to burden low- and middle-income households.

Risks Associated with Long-Term Care. Medicaid, which was among the Great Society programs of the Johnson administration, is a cost-sharing program between the federal government and the states. It covers a broad range of medical and health care services as well as long-term services and supports (LTSS). States are required to observe minimum rules of coverage and provision of services but have the option to expand both coverage and the services they provide at their own expense.

The share of the population covered by Medicaid has grown substantially over recent years. Originally, its coverage was restricted to those aged, disabled, and blind persons who had qualified for Supplementary Security Income (SSI), which was 74% of the federal poverty line in 2018. The growth in coverage reflects both the inclusion of additional elements of the population and the adoption of less-restrictive means tests. In 36 states and the District of Columbia that have opted to participate in the Affordable Care Act's expansion of Medicaid in 2015, virtually all state residents whose income does not exceed $16,750 per year for an individual as of 2018 (i.e., 138% of the federal poverty level) are covered. Consequently, virtually all Americans in these states who satisfy the program's conditions for eligibility, regardless of their age or whether or not they are disabled, have coverage under Medicaid.

The original Medicaid legislation requires all states to participate in its programs. It relied on an income test as well as an asset test to determine eligibility for both health care and LTC, which included stays not only at nursing homes but also at assisted living facilities and community-based services. The income and asset limits included in the original legislation apply to what is known as the Aged, Blind, and Disabled pathway (ABD pathway), which covers the first group to be eligible for Medicaid. The income limit equaled 74% of the federal poverty line in 2018, but some states have the option to increase the limit up to 100%. The income test excludes income from government programs as well as a small part of earned income.[17] As of 2018, the monthly income limit for all the states and the District of Columbia ranged from $528 in Connecticut to $1,164 in Hawaii for an individual, with a median value of $750, and from $696 to $1,578 for a couple, with a median value of $1,125. In about half of the states, the limit for a single person falls between $700 and $800 (Musumeci et al. 2019).

The asset limit for an individual ranges from $1,500 in New Hampshire to $7,560 in Arkansas and for a couple ranges from $1,500 in New Hampshire

[17]The limits of the income and asset tests and other limits included in this and the next two paragraphs are for the year 2015 and come from Musumeci et al. (2019). Higher disregards apply in the case of boarding homes and shared living (i.e., noninstitutional) arrangements.

to $11,340 in Arkansas. Most states impose a limit of $2,000 for individuals and $3,000 for couples.[18] The limits appear to be low, but they exclude the value of an applicant's primary residence (up to a value of $560,000, or as much as $840,000 at the option of the state), one automobile, and personal property and household belongings.[19] These exclusions effectively make the asset test a limit on financial assets, not real assets, for most older Americans. The treatment of retirement plan balances under the asset test varies from state to state: a few states exclude them entirely. Warshawsky and Marchand (2017) estimate that in 2010 some 71% of retirement plan assets were countable toward Medicaid asset tests.

For older Americans in need of long-term care (LTC), two other pathways to Medicaid eligibility are available that broaden the program's coverage considerably. The first is the special income rule, under which 42 states and the District of Columbia have chosen to increase the income limit to three times the standard payment for SSI, which amounted to three times $750 or $2,250 per month in 2018. An asset test that for most states is similar to the test for the ABD pathway also applies.[20] The income limit of the special income rule is considerably higher than the limit applying under the original program, and three of every four Americans age 65 years and older live in states that offer this pathway.[21]

The second additional avenue of eligibility is the medically needy pathway. The medically needy pathway provides some coverage for applicants whose medical expenses consume a large fraction of their income. Some 34 states have opted for this program, of which 26 have chosen also to apply the special income pathway.[22] Its income test is based on a monthly income limit that each state sets. Applicants whose income exceeds that limit are not eligible

[18]Eight states have elected an option allowing to use their own income criteria provided these are no more restrictive than what they had in place in 1972.

[19]Arizona has no limit on asset holdings for either individuals or couples.

[20]The limit is 250% of SSI in Delaware. In Missouri, it varies by program. The eight states that have not opted for the special income rule are California, Hawaii, Illinois, Montana, Nebraska, New York, North Carolina, and North Dakota. These states have all opted to participate in the medically needy pathway described next. Massachusetts does not apply the special income rule in the case of institutions (e.g., nursing homes) but does apply it for home and community-based services.

[21]In about half of the states, individuals whose income exceeds 300% of the SSI can be eligible for support from Medicaid if they establish what is known as a Miller trust, and they administer through it the income above 300% of the SSI. See Musumeci et al. (2019) for additional discussion.

[22]Some 34 states apply this pathway for pregnant women and children; 32 states apply it for seniors and the disabled (Texas and Tennessee being the exceptions); and 26 states apply it for low-income parents.

through this pathway unless they are able to show that they have incurred medical expenses that equal or exceed the difference between their current monthly income and their state's monthly limit over a stipulated period of time that ranges from one to six months depending on the state.[23] Monthly income limits for an individual in 2018 ranged from \$100 for Louisiana to \$1,041 for Vermont. The median value for an individual was \$488. Limits for a couple ranged from \$192 for Louisiana to \$1,372 for Illinois. The median for a couple was \$559.

As an example of how this rule would be applied, consider an individual applicant with a monthly income of \$2,800 who is a resident of West Virginia, where the income limit is \$200 and the budgetary period is six months. The applicant would have to incur \$15,600, or (\$2,800 – \$200) × 6, in medical expenditures to be eligible for Medicaid's coverage on additional expenditures for the remainder of the budgetary period. To take another example, suppose an individual has a monthly income of \$6,500 in a state with a monthly income limit of \$500. With a budgetary period of six months, the individual must incur medical expenses of \$36,000, or (6 × \$6,000), before Medicaid would cover excess expenditures for the reminder of the budgetary period. Once the budgetary period ends, the whole procedure must begin again. This second example makes clear that the relief the medically needy pathway offers drops significantly with increases in income.

Any American who satisfies the asset test and whose income falls below the limits set by the original Medicaid program or the special income test is effectively insured by Medicaid against the risk of requiring LTC. Nursing home residents, however, are expected to contribute most of their income to defraying the costs incurred on their behalf before Medicaid kicks in.[24] They are allowed only a small personal allowance. If only a little money is left over after the nursing home takes its share, the sharing rule may be inflicting hardship. An important issue is how much discretionary income a nursing home resident would require over and above what is needed to cover food, other basic living expenses, and the cost of care.

The fact that so many older Americans can expect to rely on financing from Medicaid should they need LTSS must reduce the incentive they have to save for their declining years. In the case of a nursing home resident with a spouse, rules are in place to avoid the spouse's impoverishment as a result

[23]Eleven states have opted for a budgetary period of one month, and 13 states have opted for six months. In several other states, the limit depends on whether the applicant plans to remain in the community (Musumeci et al. 2016, appendix table 3).

[24]Recipients of community-based services can retain much more of their income, because they will be responsible for much more of the basic costs of living (lodging, food, etc.).

of large LTSS expenditures on behalf of a chronically ill spouse. As we have discussed, older Americans who supplement their Medicare policy with a Medigap or a similar policy avoid much of the risk of catastrophic loss. The poor and even the middle class, however, still can be saddled with a substantial burden because of the cost of expensive drugs and the quirks of insurance coverage.

The financial arrangements for Medicaid's coverage of LTC differ substantially from those of Medicare's coverage of short-term illness or disability. The degree of exposure to LTC risk depends on income and the state of residence. Older Americans whose incomes are below the SSI limit and who satisfy the asset test are covered. In addition, older Americans are covered if they are a resident in 1 of the 42 states that have adopted the special income pathway,[25] have income less than three times the SSI limit, and satisfy the asset test. In the remaining eight states, the medically needy pathway also may provide relief to some, but the asset test may require a substantial spend-down.

Of the 42 states including the District of Columbia that do grant eligibility through the special income pathway, only 26 also offer eligibility through the medically needy pathway. Older Americans in the other 18 states with relatively high incomes, and without private LTC insurance, must rely entirely on their own resources to pay for LTSS.

Relying on Medicaid rather than taking out LTC insurance makes a lot of sense for older Americans with modest incomes. Note, however, that while relying on private LTC insurance requires the payment of premiums typically starting some years before need, private insurance normally pays all or most of the expenses of LTC once care begins and LTC policy holders would have more choice. Perhaps the real elephant in the room is the quality of the coverage of nursing homes by Medicaid.

If older Americans cannot qualify for LTSS coverage under Medicaid and lack private LTC insurance, what expenses would they face? A recent study reports that the probability that one or both members of a healthy 65-year-old couple will move to a nursing home at some point in their remaining lifetime is 78%; the probability of visits by a home health aide is 63%; and the probability of residing in an assisted living facility is 29% (Crook and Sutedja 2017).[26] Despite the likelihood that older Americans will need some kind of LTC, the median duration of a nursing home stay is only nine months.

[25]In Massachusetts, as noted, the special income rule covers home-based and community but not institutional care.

[26]The probabilities add up to more than 100% because a couple can experience not just one but two or all three of these states of the world.

The median duration of home health visits and residence in assisted living facilities is 14 months.

With the annual cost of a nursing home stay averaging $92,376 in 2016, the cost of long stays becomes prohibitive.[27] The chances that a nursing home stay lasts for more than one year has been estimated at 32% for at least one member of a healthy 65-year-old couple; the probability of a stay of more than three years has been estimated at 8% (Crook and Sutedja 2017). The odds that an older American who does not qualify for Medicaid will incur substantial expenses for LTC are not negligible, nor are they really large. Comparing the contingencies of a car accident and the need for LTC, it is highly unlikely that Americans can pass through life without having to deal with an auto accident of some degree of seriousness, but the probability of requiring LTC is lower. As a result, wishful thinking may lead many people to underestimate their exposure to the latter.

The older Americans who are most exposed to LTC expense risk are those who live in the 18 states that do not offer eligibility through the medically needy pathway, and whose incomes exceed the limit of three times SSI.[28] Residents of these states who are 65 years of age or older account for about 28% of the national total. Assuming, perhaps conservatively, that no more than 50% of the elder population fails this test (i.e., have income in excess of three times the SSI limit), that would amount to about 14% of the population age 65 years and older for the nation as a whole. The asset test, however, also must be met. If it cannot, then candidates for LTSS must spend down those of their assets that are deemed to be countable or protect them by means of a trust.[29]

Political Risk. The retirement prospects of the current generation of American workers undoubtedly are subject to political risk, although this risk often is not treated in the crisis literature. This particular aspect of the crisis stems from some basic demographic trends, the modalities of Social Security and Medicare/Medicaid financing, and the well-known tendency for Congress to kick the can down the road rather than address a steadily worsening situation.[30]

The Old-Age, Survivors, and Disability Insurance Programs (OASDI) are financed by the proceeds of a payroll tax, and the interest credited on the

[27]Crook and Sutedja (2017) report that costs range considerably nationwide, from $60,000 in Oklahoma to $135,000 in New York. These figures come from Genworth (2016).

[28]These calculations treat the District of Columbia as a state, making 51 states in all.

[29]For a general discussion of estate planning and the role it can play in preserving a family's assets when LTC becomes necessary, see Correia, Sayre, and Allen (2017).

[30]Turner (2017) analyzes Congressional inaction regarding Social Security reform from a behavioral economics perspective.

Trust Fund, which is built up when revenue plus interest exceed expenditure and run down when the reverse is the case. The government pays interest on the accumulated balance of the Trust Fund at a predetermined rate. There are in fact two separate programs: (1) OASI, for normal retirement and dependent survivors, and (2) DI, the government's disability insurance program.

It is not necessary—and not a clever idea—to try to balance the revenues and expenditure of either program annually. These programs are in fact outside the annual budgetary process. Most important, over an extended period of time, revenues should be sufficient to fund mandated expenditure.

In the early 1980s, following the report of the Greenspan commission, which recommended a series of gradual increases in what is known as the Full Retirement Age (FRA) from 65 years to 67 years depending on a participant's date of birth, the OASDI Trust Fund reversed its ongoing deterioration and started to accumulate surpluses. These surpluses were deemed to be necessary to handle the projected increase in population and the bulge in retirements taking place as the baby boom generation began to retire. The Early Retirement Age (ERA) remained 62, but the financial penalty for retiring early increased.

Every year, the OASDI Trustees publish a comprehensive report on OASDI finances, which is available free of charge online and in print. The report presents the complex calculations of SSA's Office of the Chief Actuary, which each year projects the system's finances out 75 years. On the revenue side, this requires projecting the number of workers subject to the SS payroll taxes for 75 years, and what is known as the taxable payroll. (In any particular year, that part of a salary that exceeds some stipulated cutoff point is not taxed, so that the taxable payroll is less than the nation's total wage and salary bill.) The ceiling for taxable wages and salaries, which in 2019 was $132,900, is indexed to the CPI for urban workers. For the purposes of the report's projections, the 6.2% payroll tax rate levied on both employers and employees is assumed not to change. (The self-employed pay both the employer and employee share.)

The format of the annual report has changed little over the years. The numbers it presents, however, have changed—that is, they have gotten worse—although the conclusions of the 2019 report are not markedly different from those of its recent predecessors (OASDI Trustees' 2019 Report). Every year, the annual report makes three sets of projections for the system's major variables—a pessimistic projection, an optimistic projection, and a middle-of-the-road or intermediate projection. In the latest report, these run from 2019 to 2093, or for 75 years. This period is required by law.

Attention normally focuses on the intermediate scenario. Particular interest is focused on the date at which the Trust Fund is exhausted. As long as the Trust Fund has money, entitlements can exceed revenues and still be paid. This feature distinguishes the US system from those of other industrial economies, although these countries may have more flexibility to tap other, nonpayroll tax revenue sources. Once the Trust Fund is exhausted, however, revenues must be increased, or there must be some combination of revenue increases and benefit cuts. The latest version of the Trustees' report projects that the Trust Fund will be exhausted in 2035 or in 16 years.

The 2019 Trustees' report calculates a purely notional estimate of what would happen to the system's unfunded obligations over a 75-year period if nothing is done to the parameters of the system given its demographic and economic assumptions. Simplifying somewhat, unfunded obligations in year $t(UO_t)$ are equal to their level of year $t-1$ accumulated at an appropriate rate of interest r_t plus the revenue-expenditure imbalance $(E_t - R_t)$ in year t:

$$UO_t = UO_{t-1}(1+r_t)+(E_t - R_t).$$

The current present value of the unfunded obligations (UO_{75}) through the year 2093, where the Trust Fund's accumulated reserves in 2018 are represented by TFR_{2018} and a constant interest rate r is assumed, can be expressed as follows:

$$UO_{75} = \sum_{i=2019}^{2093}(E_i - R_i)\big/(1+r)^i - \text{TFR}_{2018}.$$

The OASDI's actuaries calculate that the present value of the open-group unfunded obligations of the system under the intermediate scenario amounts to no less than $14.8 trillion, or close to 70% of the estimated 2018 GDP.[31] The projection period of 75 years over which this figure is derived is, of course, arbitrary; an alternative period might have been proposed. That said, acting based on calculations assuming a short period could require brutal adjustments to the system's parameters, whereas a longer period would only encourage further delay. The ideal length will discourage such shortsightedness.

Purely as an illustrative exercise, it is useful to express in simple formulaic terms the increase in the combined payroll tax that would be necessary to close the unfunded obligations gap. In choosing to focus on the payroll tax, we do not mean to imply that other measures, or a combination of a payroll

[31]With an open-group method, new workers continue to join the system and are covered. Effectively, Social Security is assumed to be a going concern.

tax hike and expenditure reduction, might not make more sense both politically and socially.

If the needed increase in the payroll tax is ΔT, the taxable payroll in year t is TP_t, and the time horizon is 75 years, then the increase in the payroll tax necessary to fill the gap will be derived from the following formula:

$$UO = \sum_{i=1}^{75} \Delta T(TP_i) \big/ (1+r)^i .$$

We describe this as a "purely illustrative" exercise because that is what it is.[32] As formulated, the whole of the system's taxable payroll is immediately subject to the increased payroll tax: not only younger workers, or workers just entering the system, but also those on the verge of retirement. The 2019 report estimates that an immediate across the board increase in the payroll tax of 22% (i.e., 2.8 percentage points) would be required to restore 75-year solvency. A cut in all benefits of 17% with no changes to the payroll tax would be required to have the same effect (Committee for a Responsible Federal Budget 2019).

Quite apart from the utter lack of political feasibility of so drastic a measure as an across-the-board increase in the payroll tax, the measure arguably would violate an informal social contract. The proposal also might be seen as unfair in that it affects only current wage earners, whereas current retirees are held harmless.[33] Workers who had been subject to the same payroll taxes for years suddenly would find themselves with what could be a burdensome increase in their payroll tax burden. Workers within a year or two of retirement might not be enormously affected because the present value of the increase in their tax burden would not be significant. It would be harder for workers in their prime earnings years to deal with the increase. Workers just entering the system, of course, would experience the biggest increase, but they would have many more years to take compensatory action and would not have become used to the existing rate structure.

[32]A similar effect might be achieved by requiring that the principal insurance amount (PIA) be calculated on the basis of more than 35 years of work, provided the number of additionally required years was sufficiently high. Currently, the calculation requires picking a worker's best 35 years (i.e., 35 years with the highest indexed wages) and dividing by 35. A worker with 33 years of contributions is said to have two "zero" years. Raising the number of required years to, say, 38 would undoubtedly increase the number of zero years and require the inclusion in the calculus of years when salaries were less high. This measure thus lowers the calculated benefit.

[33]If the disposable income of current workers declines, other things equal, but their Social Security benefit is unchanged, their savings would tend to decline to reduce the increase in the replacement rate caused by the tax hike.

The financial blow entailed by higher payroll taxes could be softened: for example, by delaying its introduction or by making the rate of increase vary with the worker's age. These palliative measures would require a higher average increase in the tax rate.

The appropriate role of adjustments to the pensions of already retired persons has always been a subject of contention in any country with a national system. Consider Greece, for example, where the normal retirement age was 50 years until the recent reforms. Attempts to change "normal" retirement ages, even when these appear to outside observers to be unrealistically low, can be met with fierce resistance.

A basic problem arises with attempts to lower the average pension of older retirees—that is, typically, they have no means of compensating for the loss in their income. Even relatively young retirees may have difficulty doing so. Although the unemployment rates of older American workers actually may be lower than those of younger workers, if they lose their job, their unemployment spells are likely to be much longer, or they simply may never rejoin the workforce. In addition, older workers tend to stop working earlier than they had expected to, in part because of unforeseen illness or job loss.[34] The risk of disability also tends to be underestimated.

Another possible economy measure might be to impose means-testing on the pension benefit. The pension benefit might be not simply a function of a worker's best 35 years of work excluding any part of a salary that exceeded the cutoff point (currently $137,700), but instead calculated as a decreasing function of the recipient's adjusted gross income from all sources. Such a measure has been discussed. Finally, note that although the Social Security pension is indexed, the index used for the annual adjustment may understate the inflation that the elderly face. Resorting to an index that tends to increase by even less than the current rate would make adjustment and reform all the more difficult. The evidence on this point is contested, however.[35]

These are only a few of the ways that the accounts of OASDI can be balanced. There may be only 50 ways to leave your lover, as Simon and Garfunkel have instructed us, but the combinations and permutations of measures to address Social Security's financial imbalance are far greater than 50, at least if political realities are ignored. All of these permutations, however, address the basic question of how the "adjustment" should be distributed among the current working generation, current retirees, and those not yet part of the system. Within those three broad categories, a similar question of who should bear the burden arises.

---

[34]For a recent discussion of these issues, see Simon (2018).

[35]See Munnell and Chen (2015).

How does political risk compare in predictability and in its incidence across different age and income groups? The oldest of the current generation of retirees will not be affected. This is not necessarily the case with investment risk, longevity risk, or medical and LTC cost risk. Political risk for those workers who are comparatively old but still accumulating retirement savings may be tempered by the political difficulty of targeting this group. That leaves the young workers and future labor market participants.

In addition to the basic issue of who will take the hit, there is the other issue of the timing of any measure or set of measures to address Social Security's imbalance. The day is not far off when the Trust Fund will be reduced to zero, but some years remain before that event, and the projections of the Annual Report conceivably could be too pessimistic. All this suggests that political risk is of greatest concern to younger workers.

Congress still has some discretion about when it would pass new measures. Moreover, no law says that the set of measures passed must eliminate the projected unfunded liabilities over the next 75 years. Congress should choose a shorter period: for example, it might obtain an estimate of the unfunded obligations that would be accumulated over the next 25 years. This would require, however, a further set of measures to be taken in the future.

Social Security is not the only source of political risk. Medicare and Medicaid are huge entitlement programs, with rapidly rising expenditures and ballooning deficits.[36] Reform of all of these programs is politically difficult, and in the case of Medicare and Medicaid, reform is further hampered by the difficulty of calculating the effects of reform given the particular challenge of predicting health cost inflation. It is possible, however, to imagine measures that affect the cost of medical care favorably, whereas the income needs of retirees cannot easily be managed that way.

It is hard to be specific about the incidence and severity of political risk, but this risk cannot be ignored. Failing to address this risk simply creates more uncertainty for Americans who already are retired and increases uncertainty even more for workers still saving for retirement.

[36]The two Health Insurance (HI) trust funds that finance Medicare are projected to run actuarial deficits on an annual basis of 0.91% of taxable payroll over the 75-year projection period, compared with 2.78% of taxable payroll for the combined OASDI trust funds (Social Security Administration 2019). A payroll tax of 2.6% split evenly between employers and employees, the premiums paid by beneficiaries, and general tax revenues are the main sources of finance for the trust funds.

3. The Debate

This chapter presents the opposing views of the most insightful or better-known analysts and researchers who have tackled the crisis issue. Its coverage is not exhaustive, but in the author's view, the studies it reviews cover the most important of the analytical approaches to the issue.

The Crisis Advocates

Nari Rhee and Other Researchers Associated with the National Institute on Retirement Security. We can study in depth only a few examples drawn from the set of crisis advocates. Those whose work we describe here vary considerably in the way they have addressed the basic question of whether or not a retirement crisis exists. Nari Rhee and other researchers associated with the National Institute on Retirement Security (NIRS), a Washington think tank, have not relied on an elaborate model of saving and retirement risks. Instead, they have emphasized the skimpiness of retirement plan balances held by a large share of households relative to these households' estimated retirement income needs, combined with age-specific targets for the ratio of assets to income that are derived from a target replacement ratio. Given limited data and research resources, this may be the best way to assess the problem.

Without relying on an elaborate model, Rhee has argued that most households, including many who are still some years from retirement, have a wealth-to-income ratio so low that they either will fail to have a financially secure retirement or will have to save an implausibly large share of income to build up their assets to a level at which they can achieve one. This is true of both younger households and households approaching retirement.

Rhee (2013) reviews the evidence on holdings of retirement accounts, basing her observations on the Federal Reserve's triennial Survey of Consumer Finances (hereafter referred to as the SCF). The results of the SCF 2013 survey had not yet been released at the time of writing, and Rhee has based her evaluation on data from the 2010 survey. An update published in 2015 is able to use data from the 2013 SCF, but it arrives at similar conclusions (Boivie and Rhee 2015).

Rhee's findings are similar to those of a number of other researchers: only about half of the workforce has a retirement account (including 401(k) plans, traditional and Roth IRAs, 403(b) and 457(b) accounts, and Simple IRAs); the median balances of these accounts are low; and the size of holdings as well as the degree of participation in plans is strongly related to income.

The median retirement balance for households with a head age 55 to 64 years old (including households both with and without retirement accounts) is only $12,000. The median balance for those households in that group with a retirement saving account is $100,000 (see **Table 2**). The means are much higher, reflecting a highly skewed wealth distribution.

To derive an indicator of retirement adequacy, Rhee (2013) takes estimates of household income from the SCF for those households with income in the range of $5,000 to $499,999 in the latest year that was available (2010) when she was writing. She multiplies these estimates by age-related targets to calculate the financial wealth-to-income ratio, which she takes from a 2012 study by Fidelity (see **Table 3**). These ratios reach a maximum of eight times income at age 67. (This is a low target, and given the decline in interest rates

Table 2. Retirement Account Assets, All Households and Those with Accounts, by Age of Household Head (median value in 2010 dollars)

Age of Household Head	All Households	Those with Retirement Accounts
25–34	—	13,000
35–44	1,400	31,000
45–54	10,100	60,000
55–64	12,000	100,000
25–64	3,000	40,000

Source: Rhee (2013).

Table 3. Savings Target as a Multiple of Current Income by Age

Age	Multiple of Income
25	—
30	0.5
35	1.0
40	2.0
45	3.0
50	4.0
55	5.0
60	6.0
65	7.0
67	8.0

Source: Fidelity (2012).

since the NIRS studies, the target probably should be higher, as a more recent position paper from Fidelity (2018) indicates.

A household is deemed to be on track if its savings-to-income ratio has reached the level shown in Table 3 conditional on the age of the household head: for example, those households with a head age 50 should have a wealth-to-income ratio of at least 4. The wealth-to-income ratios shown in Table 3 do not reflect the capitalized value of Social Security. The replacement rate from Social Security alone is assumed to be 35% for all households.

The wealth-to-income targets are compared with wealth-to-income ratios derived from the SCF's estimates of households' actual wealth, which for households with heads from 25 to 64 years of age are measured in four different ways: (1) the sum of retirement account balances, (2) total retirement assets (which include the capitalized value of DB plans), (3) total financial assets, and (4) net worth (which includes housing equity but unlike the other measures is net of debt). These ratios are calculated for each household, and a distribution across households is derived, an exercise that produces some dismal estimates, as reported in Rhee (2013): using retirement account balances alone as the measure of retirement wealth, some 92% of households come up short; using net worth, 65% come up short (see **Table 4**).[37] Even more remarkable are the estimates by age-group: 95.4% of households with a head age 55 to 64 years old fall short when retirement account balances are used; 67.8% of that group fail the test when net worth is used. The extent of the shortfall by each of these yardsticks—the depth of the shortfall of assets at retirement—is not reported.[38]

It is unclear which of the four measures of wealth is best. To the extent that home equity cannot be tapped, the use of net worth may be problematic. The denominator of the replacement ratios used here excludes in-kind income from home ownership. The other measures also present a difficulty, in that they are not net of liabilities. Other things being equal, correcting for the failure to rely on a measure of net instead of gross assets, the estimated shortfalls will increase.

At first blush, these projections would suggest that the lot of those households nearing retirement must be grim. In the case of households with low

[37]The 2015 update reports a slightly higher figure of 66.2%.

[38]A comparison can be made between measures of retirement income shortfalls and the reporting of the poverty rate. The so-called poverty head count measures the percentage of households whose income falls below the stipulated poverty line given their family size; it does not measure the depth of poverty. Many families might be poor but have incomes that were not in fact far below the poverty line. Poverty measures are also sensitive to the extent to which income (both in cash and in-kind) from transfer programs is included.

Table 4. Share of Households by Age of Household Head That Fall Short of Retirement Saving Target Using Various Wealth Measures (in percent)

	Measure of Wealth			
Age of Household Head	Retirement Account Balances	Total Retirement Assets	Total Financial Assets	Net Worth
25–34	80.3	76.0	65.8	51.1
35–44	95.3	93.0	89.8	70.1
45–54	96.8	94.5	93.3	69.8
55–64	95.4	93.2	88.8	67.8
25–64	92.0	90.0	84.0	65.0

Note: Figures for 25–64 total are rounded to the nearest integer.
Source: Rhee (2013).

incomes, Social Security can provide a relatively high replacement rate, one that is higher than the study's assumed estimate. Even so, the additional savings needed at retirement to generate the income that will bring the replacement rate up to its conventional range is a fairly large multiple of income.[39]

Rhee's pessimistic prognosis rests on two strong assumptions: a target replacement rate of 85%, which derives from the study by Aon Hewitt (2012) discussed next, and the assumed relationship between age and the ratio of some measure of savings to income (hereafter called the income multiple). The income multiple actually needed to maintain the same standard of living in retirement should be somewhat lower, because it should allow for the possible impact on a household's expenditure of the empty nest and the winding down of expenditures that have a more or less fixed term, like paying off a mortgage or paying for college. Basing the estimate of income to be replaced on a single year also could be problematic. A spike in income at the end of working life would exaggerate any shortfall in wealth needed to achieve an adequate standard of living in retirement if the retiree was using a period like five years at the end of working life as the basis for calculating the income needed in retirement. In principle at least, retirement income advisers should consider these effects.

The treatment of housing equity is uncertain. Equity would be included in a measure of net worth and in any case the income in kind from home ownership really should be included in measures of both working and retirement income. If, instead, net or gross financial assets are used as the measure

[39]For a household with an annual income of $60,000—which is a little above the median for age 60–65—the Social Security retirement benefit (assuming that the AIME used to calculate the benefit is also $60,000) will equal $24,949, implying a replacement rate of 42%.

of accumulated saving, housing equity is effectively disregarded. It bears repeating, however, that a household that owns its home is obviously better prepared for retirement than another household with the same income that rents an identical home in a similar neighborhood.

Rhee assumes that the wealth-to-income ratio will take rise mechanically as the future retiree ages; Schieber (2015) has argued that this assumption implies a pattern of saving that is atypical. His argument is taken up again in the following section. A related issue is that the saving rate needed to achieve the wealth-to-income targets given in Table 3 might be so high that consumption in retirement would exceed the severely constrained consumption that would become necessary during the remaining period of work.

The behavior over time of measures of the wealth-to-income ratio might be interpreted to imply that, if nothing else, the cohort of recent retirees is not noticeably worse off than earlier cohorts. Specifically, data from successive waves of the SCF show that median net-worth-to-income ratios for the older age cohorts rose substantially from 1989 to 2007 before being pulled down by the sharp decline in real property values in 2010. Most of the drop in net worth is accounted for by the behavior of real assets (see **Table 5**): Nonetheless, the net worth ratios for the three age-groups shown were close to their 1989 values, increasing for the 55 to 64 and the 75 and older age-groups and declining somewhat for the 65 to 74 age-group.

Table 5. Median Wealth-to-Income Ratios, Select Age-Groups

	Age Range								
	55–64	65–74	75+	55–64	65–74	75+	55–64	65–74	75+
Year	Financial Assets			Total Assets			Net Worth		
1989	0.57	0.93	1.36	3.93	4.84	5.76	3.18	4.61	5.70
1992	0.72	0.99	1.08	4.17	5.58	6.17	3.51	5.21	5.86
1995	0.68	0.92	1.16	4.30	6.13	6.72	3.42	5.90	5.66
1998	0.96	1.60	1.61	4.39	6.39	7.03	3.62	5.95	6.48
2001	1.12	1.48	1.97	5.02	6.64	7.86	4.06	6.56	7.62
2004	1.00	0.79	1.25	5.17	6.64	7.54	4.10	6.01	7.12
2007	1.12	1.33	1.52	5.75	7.10	8.83	4.48	5.98	8.69
2010	0.81	0.86	1.18	4.79	5.81	7.05	3.34	4.97	6.51
2013	0.69	1.18	0.95	4.30	6.01	6.58	2.84	4.72	5.88
2016	0.85	1.09	1.40	4.48	5.45	7.22	3.29	4.32	6.81

Source: SCF and author's calculations. The sample size for the 75 and older households is small.

That said, the ongoing increase in longevity means that a wealth-to-income ratio that would have maintained consumption in retirement at its working-life level throughout retirement with a given probability in 1989 would no longer do that in 2016. Other changes in the economic and financial environment, such as the decline in interest rates, also probably would have worked to increase the wealth-to-income ratio needed to sustain a given replacement rate. We return to this issue in Chapter 5.

Aon Hewitt. Aon Hewitt conducted a survey of 2.2 million employees from 78 corporations in 2011 to assess their readiness for retirement. The results are reported in Aon Hewitt (2012). Their study focused on "full-career contributing employees," meaning employees who could be expected to stay in their jobs for 30 years, and who were contributing to an employer-provided retirement plan, but it also covered part-time and fixed-term employees as well as noncontributing employees.

The study's basic approach was to estimate a target for the replacement rate, and then to determine whether an employee's assets as projected to age 65, the assumed age of retirement, would be sufficient to generate the income in retirement consistent with the targeted replacement rate. Salary and savings were projected forward for each employee from age at the time of the survey to the age of 65.

The study assumes that wages and salaries grow by 1% per year in real terms for the rest of a worker's career, and the replacement rate was applied to income in the last year of work, rather than to an average of some specified number of years at end-career. Data were available or were estimated for the balances in employees' defined contribution (DC) plans and the capitalized value of DB pension plans, when employees had one or more of these plans. Saving was projected on the basis of the employee's rate of contribution to a DC plan, and a real rate of return of 2.5% was assumed for financial assets.

A replacement rate of 85%, an average rate for the population of employees, was assumed. The replacement rates from which the average was derived were determined by calculating the income in retirement that would maintain a worker's standard of living, considering the impact of income taxes and pension contributions on spendable income. This rate assumes that certain expenditure categories would decline in real terms in retirement, but that health care expenditure would increase. For example, a hypothetical employee is a 40-year-old male who has a gross salary of $60,000 and a projected salary of $160,000 at retirement with 1% real salary growth per year between age 40 and retirement. His nonmedical expenditure would decline in the first retirement year by $3,600, but his medical expenditure would increase by $7,300

(Aon Hewitt 2012, p. 14). This increase may reflect the ending of employer-provided health insurance upon retirement.[40]

The capitalized value of Social Security is assumed to be 4.9 times income. According to this study, private resources must then amount to 11 times income to avoid a shortfall. Specifically, assets at this level are needed to sustain income in retirement from age 65 to age 87 for men and to age 88 for women. This difference does not reflect the difference in male-female life expectancy at age 65.

The conclusions of the Aon Hewitt study are pretty alarming. It finds that the ratio of net assets to final salary is below the target value of 11 for 71% of full-career contributing employees; this ratio, given the study's assumptions, would sustain a replacement rate of 85% for the period of 21 or 22 years starting at a retirement age of 65. No fewer than 37% of full-career consulting employees have wealth shortfalls of more than four times final salary. This shortfall occurs in spite of the fact that most of the employees in this group are contributing to a plan. The shortfalls of noncontributors are so large that it would be impossible for most noncontributors to make up the difference.

The dismal conclusions of the Aon Hewitt study reflect to a large extent the assumptions it makes. Using income in the last year of work as the denominator, and assuming a steady increase in income during remaining working life, means that the estimated replacement rate will remain lower than it would if an income average were used.

More important, the Aon Hewitt study does not account for nonemployer-sponsored saving or home equity. It also fails to consider an employee's family situation. A large share of its sample presumably would be married or cohabiting, and the financial situation of the household would not necessarily be reflected in the apparent situation of just one of its members. The assumed capitalized value of Social Security of 4.9 times income would be quite inaccurate for employees at the extreme ends of the income distribution.

A study should not be judged adversely just because its conclusions seem outlandish. The conclusion of this study, however, that almost three-quarters of a group of comparatively affluent workers will end up underwater in retirement, should arouse some skepticism. A similar observation is warranted regarding some of the conclusions of the NIRS study.

---

[40]A similar approach to the calculation of replacement rates was used by Alicia Munnell and her colleagues at the CRR, except that the CRR uses estimates for the replacement rates of different classes of households to determine whether the household will fall short of its replacement rate.

The Center for Retirement Research at Boston College. Alicia Munnell and her colleagues at the Center for Retirement Research (CRR) at Boston College have constructed an elaborate model to calculate what they have named the National Retirement Risk Index (NRRI). The CRR's model was rolled out in 2006. It has been revised since then, notably to account for the risk of needing LTC, although its basic structure has not changed much. The NRRI model is based on SCF data, with Social Security data being used for wage and salary income.

The goal of the model is to assess the readiness for retirement of working Americans, both those nearing retirement and those still some way off. It does this (as shall be explained at greater length in this section) by comparing a projection of income in retirement with an estimate of the income needed to maintain consumption in retirement at the level attained during working life. It makes this comparison for each household interviewed by the SCF. The NRRI calculates the share of households whose projected income in retirement is more than 10% below the estimated target. In 1989 (the first year when data were collected by the SCF), the share of households at risk by this standard was 30%; by 2001, the share at risk had risen to 38%; and by 2013, it had risen to 52% (Munnell, Hou, and Webb 2015). A key issue is how great the shortfall beyond 10% is for each household finding itself under water.

Working-life income consists of wage and salary income plus income from assets, which is assumed to be 4% of total household assets. Income in retirement includes pension income, Social Security benefits, and investment income. Retirees must be 65 years of age or older if single. The older member of a couple is assumed to retire at that age as well, and the partner is assumed to retire when the older member does, with a minimum age of 62. Retired people are assumed not to work, on the grounds that the rapid decline in participation rates among older Americans as they age makes not working a plausible approximation of reality. That said, the share of older Americans working beyond the conventional retirement age is on the rise.

The CRR estimates lifetime wages and salaries by starting with an estimate of the current wage for each working member of a household from the SCF. The SCF does not produce a time series of wages for each working member of a household, so its estimate for the survey year for a given household is extrapolated backward using historical data on wages from the Social Security Administration (SSA). Someone reporting no earnings is assumed to have no earnings back to the end date of last employment, a date that is reported to the SCF. Because the SSA's wage profiles do not allow for years of zero earnings, zero earnings years are assigned randomly. The last step is to inflate the historical series of estimated wages and salaries using an economy-wide wage index, and then to calculate an average indexed wage over the individual's working life. This has the effect of increasing that person's average wage above what it would be if it were indexed to consumer prices, thereby lowering the calculated replacement ratio (see Chapter 2).

These estimates and projections are the basis for the model's projection of Social Security benefits. Average indexed monthly earnings (AIME) are calculated by taking the 35 best years of a worker's indexed wages, as Social Security does. The principal insurance amount (PIA) is calculated by applying the SSA's formula.[41] Single people and the older member of a couple are assumed to claim their Social Security benefit when they retire.

Estimates of the ratio of financial assets and housing wealth to income are derived from the SCF's estimates in its successive surveys. A study of the SCF's data on wealth not only shows that the ratio of financial assets to income increases with the age of the household head, as could be expected, but also shows that the ratios have not changed enormously (see **Figure 1**) from one survey to the other (the survey is conducted triennially) and, in particular, have not displayed a trend.

Estimates of the ratio for four components of wealth—401(k) holdings, other financial assets, gross housing wealth, and net housing wealth—are derived for each household by estimating an equation for each component, with two independent variables: a dummy variable for the household's age cohort, and a variable for the age of the head of household. The equation is estimated for three subgroups—the top, middle, and bottom third of the income distribution—and is projected to age 62.[42,43] These equations are used

[41]As of 2019, Social Security replaces 90% of the first $926 of monthly indexed wages; the next $4,657 is replaced at a rate of 32%. A rate of 15% applies to the next (i.e., highest) salary tranche. There is no benefit related to the part of income above which Social Security tax was not due.

[42]The equation for the ratio of wealth to income for each asset class (WR) is written in Munnell et al. (2006) like this: $WR_i = a + \sum_{j=1}^{20} b_j COHORT_{ij} + \sum_{k=1}^{10} c_k AGEIND_{ik}$.
The COHORT variable represents 20 birth cohorts, from 1918–1920 to 1978–1980. The survivors of the 1918–1920 birth cohort would have been 69–71 years old at the time of the first survey in 1989. There are ten specified age ranges: 30–32, 33–35, 36–38, 39–41 … and 57–59. A household head's age determines the values of the ten age indicator variables. The greater the age of the head of household the greater is the value of the sum of the ten variables. In the case of a household head age 30 or under, $AGEIND_k$ has a value of zero for each $AGEIND_k$ from k equals 1 to 10. In the case of a household head age 70, each of the 10 elements would have a value of three.

[43]The relationship between income (Y) and wages (W) can be derived from the equation $Y = W + rA$, where r is the return on assets (A). The projected ratio of assets to income is a constant for a household of a given age and cohort membership: $A/Y = k$, where k is a constant. It follows that $Y = W/(1 - rk)$.

Figure 1. Median Wealth-to-Income Ratios by Age of Household Head

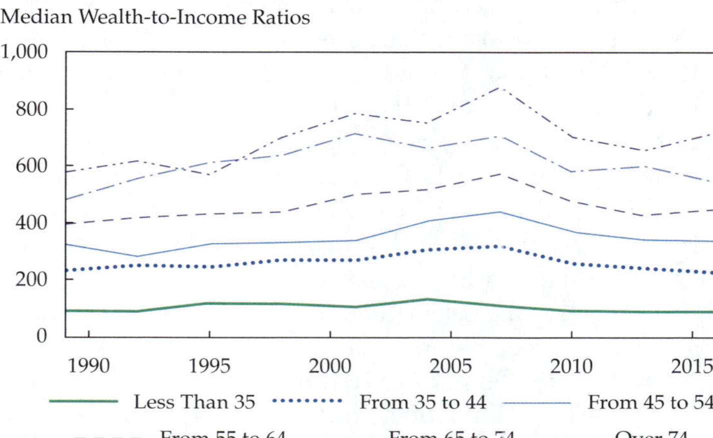

Note: Data collected from the Federal Reserve's triennial Survey of Consumer Finances.

to project wealth-to-asset ratios through age 62.[44] If a household's actual ratio is below the ratio projected for that age and cohort, the gap is maintained in projecting the ratio to age 62. For example, if a household had a wealth-to-income ratio of 1.3 at age 50 when the average ratio for households with heads age 50 in that particular birth cohort was 1.5, the ratio projected for the household at age 62 would be 1.3 divided by 1.5 times the average at age 62.

The NRRI model also projects the ratio of housing wealth to income. The imputed rental income on a house and the "reversionary interest" (basically, the value of the house that could be unlocked by an RM) is calculated at age 62. The reversionary interest minus any outstanding mortgage is annuitized and included in the estimate of the household's retirement income. The imputed rent on the house is included in both retirement income and working income, as it should be. As of 2006, when the paper was written, the potential value of an RM was about 45% of the value of a house. The sum total of a household's wealth at age 62 is assumed to be used to buy an inflation-indexed annuity. Although few households actually buy an annuity, the income that could be derived in this way may be a good measure of the household's financial condition.

[44]The decision to truncate the estimation of wealth-to-income ratios at age 62 was made because of the tendency for income to decline by large and unstable amounts between 62 and 65.

The sum of wages and asset income during working life, plus imputed rent, is used as the denominator of replacement rate calculations; the sum of postretirement asset income, Social Security, and DB pension income if any, plus imputed rent and reversionary income, is used as the numerator. The authors found in 2006 that early baby boomers had replacement rates higher than those of late boomers and Gen Xers regardless of their income level. This may reflect, in part, the fact the baby boomers began buying stocks in the 1970s and 1980s, when stock market prices were relatively low. Unsurprisingly, households with a DB pension had higher replacement rates than households with only a DC pension or no pension.

The NRRI requires the calculation of a target replacement rate that can be compared with the model's projected rates. The target replacement rate is calculated by first making an indirect estimate of consumption during working life. This is done by subtracting, from income, the income taxes paid to all levels of government; saving; and mortgage payments (see **Table 6** for an example). To derive the target replacement rate, consumption in retirement is set equal to that number. Then, income in retirement is set equal to the amount, including taxes, that would be consistent with that number.[45] Separate calculations are made for one- and two-earner couples, for single people, for households with and without DB pension plans, and for homeowning and nonhomeowning households as well as for three earnings levels. (Replacement rates were not calculated for every household in the SCF's sample, but rather were calculated for representative households.)

According to the authors, because a high share of income in retirement for low-income households comes from Social Security, these households do not need to save as much as higher-income households. Because their saving is lower in working life, their targeted replacement rates will be higher than the replacement rates of wealthier households.

The original version of the CRR's model treated medical expenditure as discretionary. Thus, in determining the replacement rate, medical expenditure was included with all nonmedical expenditure, and the replacement rate target was based on an estimate of expenditure that would include medical expenditure. As explained in Munnell et al. (2009), medical expenditure is now treated as a necessary expenditure category. Medical expenditure in retirement is programmed and assumed to equal the sum of Medicare and Medigap premiums and estimated OOP expenditure. The target for nonmedical expenditure in retirement is set to equal its average level during working

[45]Some income in retirement, like the Social Security benefit and income, if any, from a defined benefit pension, is already determined. Other income then is set equal to ensure that there is enough total income to finance the target for consumption in retirement.

Table 6. Illustration of the Derivation of a Target Replacement Rate Given Average Income, Outlays, and Consumption During Working Life (in current dollars)

Income	
Earnings	59,000
Imputed rent net of mortgage interest	500
Net investment income	1,600
Total working-life income	61,100
Working-life outlays excluding consumption	15,700
Mortgage principal repayments	2,600
Saving	800
Taxes	12,300
Working-life consumption (income minus outlays excluding consumption)	45,400
Retirement income	
Social Security	24,500
Imputed rent	2,860
Reversionary interest	3,300
Annuity	3,840
Other income including pensions	11,900
Total retirement income	46,400
Outlays (taxes) excluding consumption	1,000
Retirement consumption (Retirement income minus outlays excluding consumption)	45,400
Target replacement rate	76%

Source: Author's calculations, based on Tables B-1 and B-2 in Munnell et al. (2006).

life. This change has the effect of reducing the budget available for nonmedical expenditure, and therefore, it increases the percentage of households that fall short of the NRRI's targets.

LTC expenditure, which previously has not been considered explicitly, is now assumed to be financed, if only partially, by an RM on the principal residence or by the purchase of LTC insurance (which most households in fact lack). Because this reversionary interest previously was used to finance other expenditures, financing LTC with an RM has the effect of increasing the share of households under water, according to the NRRI's criterion. In 2009, the increase in that share resulting from the combined effect of the change in the treatment of medical expenditure and LTC was calculated to be 21 percentage points (an increase from 44% to 65%). Neither medical nor LTC costs is determined stochastically, although both are explicitly recognized by the model.

The Retirement Security Projection Model (Employee Benefit Research Institute). The Retirement Security Projection Model (RSPM), which was developed by Jack VanDerhei and Craig Copeland at Employee Benefit Research Institute (EBRI), is a complex micro-simulation model that can be used for a variety of policy simulations. The simulation began life in 1999 as a project for the state of Oregon to assess the preparedness of its residents for retirement. The RSPM has since been used in a number of other states with the same end in mind. The model has relied on the stochastic treatment of major postretirement risks, such as longevity risk, postretirement investment risk, and the risk of needing LTC. It is used to calculate what EBRI has termed "Retirement Readiness Ratings." By 2003, the RSPM had become a national model and was being used to conduct policy experiments.[46]

EBRI publishes frequent issue briefs reporting on analysis and policy experiments conducted using the RSPM. For example, in VanDerhei and Copeland (2010), the model is used to simulate (1) the impact of autoenrollment and autoescalation of employee contribution rates in 401(k) plans, (2) the percentage of the population at risk for inadequate retirement income by age cohort and income group, (3) the impact of years of eligibility for participation in a DC plan on the population at risk for an inadequate retirement, and (4) the impact of reductions in Social Security benefits on the retirement readiness of different income levels and age cohorts. This work thus recognizes political risk.

The original model was based on a time series databank of information on several million 401(k) plan participants with data going back to 1996 and on tens of thousands of 401(k) plans. An additional databank of plan descriptions is used to provide a sample of different designs of DC and DB plans. This information is combined with data from three public surveys based on self-reporting and is used to model plan participation, wages, and initial account

[46]Most of the description of the Retirement Security Projection Model that follows is taken from VanDerhei and Copeland (2010) and VanDerhei (2018).

balances as well as plan accruals (in the case of DB plans). Asset allocation information is derived from the EBRI/ICI Participant-Directed Retirement Plan Data Collection Project. Contributions to 401(k) plans are modeled to reflect the presence or absence of autoenrollment. IRA balances are derived from public surveys.[47]

The impact of job changes or job loss is captured by a stochastic job duration algorithm. The model simulates whether or not a separating employee who starts work with a new employer joins an employer-provided plan, and if so, what type of plan. Rollovers of 401(k) plan balances into IRAs are modeled using industry data. Data are also used to model the decision to leave the balances of employer-provided plans with the employer.

Income in retirement is assumed to equal the sum of the Social Security benefit and income from DB pensions, if any. Earnings on DC plans, the income from other financial assets, and withdrawals of capital are used, if necessary, to bridge any gap between the income from pensions and Social Security and projected basic expenditure.

The basic test of retirement preparedness employed by this model is whether a household is able to finance what is termed a basic level of expenditure. To determine that level, expenditure is divided into deterministic and stochastic components. The predictable part of health expenditures, which includes Medicare and Medigap premiums, is part of the deterministic component of expenditure along with OOP medical expenditure. The model assumes that all Americans age 65 and older are covered by both Medicare and Medigap. In practice, about six of every seven Medicare beneficiaries have some kind of supplemental policy, including Medigap (see Chapter 2). This assumption means that health expenditure, excluding LTC, is reasonably predictable. Nonetheless, the combined cost of Medicare and a gap policy still can be substantial. Although Medicare Part D provides for a very low copay once an insured's copayments reach a certain level, the copay is high enough that the need for expensive drugs can be burdensome to low- and middle-income households.

The benchmark level of expenditure in retirement for deterministic expenses is calculated for households of elderly Americans from the Consumer Expenditure Survey for 2008. (Values for subsequent years are calculated by applying the urban CPI to the estimates for 2008.) A single-expenditure estimate is calculated for households from three different income groups (in 2008 dollars): those with income less than $20,000; those with income between $20,000 and $39,999; and those with income of $40,000 or more.

[47]For a fuller account of the modeling of plan participation and plan contributions, see VanDerhei and Copeland (2010), in particular, the appendix.

The stochastic component of expenditure is determined by simulating LTC expenditure, including community-based services. The simulation is based on a model of the probability that in a given year an elderly American will be in one of four states: not needing LTC; needing care in a nursing home; needing community-based care (such as in-home care); or dead. Should someone move to a nursing home, the length of stay will be determined randomly, and the cost will equal the number of days times a fixed per diem. If an individual in need of LTC qualifies for Medicaid by passing the program's income and asset tests, that is accounted for in determining the cost borne by that individual. Estimates of wage and salary income are based on gender and education profiles from the Current Population Survey.

Although the model can be used to calculate replacement rates, it does not rely in its assessment of retirement readiness on a comparison of projected replacement rates with target replacement rates as the NRRI or the CRR does. Instead, the EBRI model calculates the probability that a household will run short of money (when a household's income falls short of the basic or average expenditure calculated for its income bracket, and it no longer has any assets on which it can draw to make up for the shortfall).[48] LTC costs, investment returns, and longevity are all stochastic variables. The longevity variable is based on general mortality tables. As might be expected, longevity has a major impact on outcomes. A household may avoid running out of money if its members die prematurely.

The model also can be used to calculate the probability of a shortfall in income that exceeds a given percentage of the expenditure target in a given year. One possible shortcoming of the model is that it is easier (in simulation) for a household near the top of its income range to meet its minimum calculated expenditure. For example, a household with an income of $39,500, which falls in the second income range, should have an easier time sustaining the minimum expenditure determined for its group than a household earning $20,500, which also falls in that range. Similarly, a household earning $100,000, in the third range, is less challenged by the minimum expenditure determined for its range than a household earning $41,000.

Like a financial asset, home equity can be used to plug the gap between the minimum expenditure figure and available income. The EBRI model

[48]VanDerhei (2014b) offers three reasons for EBRI's decision to eschew the replacement rate approach: (1) the limited annuitization of wealth at retirement means that relying on replacement rates takes no account of the risk of running short of money; (2) the difficulty of modeling the price of annuities given the role of risky assets in financing them; and (3) the difficulty of handling the risk of needing LTC with a replacement rate approach when few households ultimately need LTC.

has treated home equity in a number of ways: (1) the sale of the home can be simply ruled out, perhaps on the ground that home equity should be reserved to finance LTC or some other serious contingency; (2) the house can be sold once all other assets are exhausted; and (3) it can be sold with the proceeds used to finance the purchase of an annuity. The model has been used to simulate the effect on retirement preparedness of all three strategies, with the assumption that, in the last two, the household becomes a renter of housing once the house is sold. (The members of the household have to live somewhere, although they might save money by moving in with relatives.) No one strategy emerges as obviously superior to the other two. In the case of relatively young households, who would have to be in difficult straits to even contemplate this expedient, relatively little can be gained from selling the primary residence and moving into a rental accommodation. Downsizing might be an option, however.

The assumption of 100% coverage by Medicare and Medigap definitely reduces the uncertainty that could attach to medical expenditure, although uncertainty remains regarding the actual premiums, and OOP expenditure can vary substantially, although it is predetermined in EBRI's model. Longevity risk, however, has a strong influence on the risk of inadequate retirement income. The RSPM does not assume that all financial assets are annuitized, and in this respect, it accurately reflects the lack of interest older Americans have in life annuities. The difference in outcomes between older people who survive to well above the average for their age cohort and those who die relatively young is striking. In the case of the lowest income quartile, a 2014 simulation of the RSPM finds that even someone dying in the lowest longevity quartile has only a 37% chance of *not* running short of money. Someone in the fourth quartile (among those who die last) has virtually no chance of not running out of money (VanDerhei 2014a).

A recent simulation exercise (VanDerhei 2014b) illustrates how the cost of LTC can affect retirement security. If it is assumed that retirees are 100% responsible for the cost of LTC, which as explained previously is determined by multiplying a randomly determined length of stay in days in a nursing home times a predetermined daily charge, then retirees in the first (lowest) income quartile who retire at age 65 have a more than 60% chance of running short of money by age 80 and a more than 80% chance by age 100 (if they live that long).

If relieved of the responsibility for LTC, that probability drops to about 70%. In the case of the second income quartile, that probability is reduced from close to 50% to 20%. In the case of the third and fourth income quartiles, the probability of running short of money drops from 30% to less than

10% and from about 10% to negligible (see **Table 7**). Even if low- and middle-income households were relieved of the need to finance LTC, EBRI's model finds that the odds are largely stacked against them. For the cohorts approaching retirement, a recent run of the simulation model finds that about 45% are simulated to run short of money in retirement (VanDerhei 2014a).

Another issue that arises in this simulation is the likelihood of an older American bearing all or most of the cost of LTC. Even if nursing home and home health care costs are ignored, the RSPM's projections imply that the position of the bottom half of the population of older Americans is tenuous, especially those in the bottom income quartile. EBRI finds that the greater the number of years of participation in a DC plan, the lower the risk of going broke.

The importance of longevity is undeniable. The question arises whether longevity insurance in one form or another can become a more important part of the retiree's landscape. Given the relationship between income levels and longevity, it appears that the predicament of poor households that have not saved enough for retirement is relieved by the increased chances of early death. Longevity, however, like the need for a nursing home, is hard to predict, and counting on an early demise is hardly a winning strategy. The vulnerability of this quartile is somewhat ameliorated by the annuitized payout

Table 7. Probability That Baby Boomers and Gen Xers Will Run Short of Money by Indicated Year of Retirement, by Income Quartile (in percent of cohort)

Income Quartile	10th Year of Retirement (age 75)	20th Year of Retirement (age 85)	35th Year of Retirement (age 100)
Assuming LTC entirely covered by retiree			
First	72	81	83
Second	19	38	47
Third	7	19	28
Fourth	2	8	13
Assuming LTC not covered by retiree			
First	64	69	70
Second	11	17	20
Third	3	5	6
Fourth	1	1	1

Note: Retirement takes place at age 65, and survival to indicated year is assumed.
Source: VanDerhei (2014b).

of Social Security, which makes up a large portion of retirement income for this quartile and by public assistance (Medicaid) for LTC.

Gaobo Pang and Mark Warshawsky. Gaobo Pang and Mark Warshawsky (2009, 2014) adopt a somewhat-different approach in their investigation of retirement preparedness, one that is influenced by Scholz, Seshadri, and Khitatrakun (2006). (The latter study is discussed in the section "The Crisis Skeptics.") The approach by Pang and Warshawsky (2014) is based on an application of the life-cycle framework, in which the household's goal is to optimize the distribution of consumption over its lifetime. In practice, this means that consumption should not fluctuate substantially from one year to the next.

The authors divide household consumption into two parts: (1) age and work-related expenditure, and (2) what they term "other discretionary expenditure." The first category, which they call life-cycle expenditure, includes food, clothing, commuting, health care, and mortgage expenditure. Each is determined by household income, age, educational attainment, and certain other demographic variables. Separate equations are estimated for workers and for retirees. The authors note that these expenditures tend to follow a hump-shaped pattern, first rising then falling.

These expenditure categories are not determined as the result of an optimization process, but other discretionary expenditure, the residual category, is. Specifically, optimization requires that the saving rate pre- and postretirement be determined so that this expenditure category is the same in both periods. This approach effectively treats life-cycle expenditure as necessary, which is how the CRR model treats medical expenditure. Given that the pattern of life-cycle expenditure is determined by income, age, and so forth, only the distribution of other discretionary expenditure affects the optimum.

Having developed their theoretical framework, the authors then conduct an optimizing exercise using data from the SCF 2010. They include in their sample workers age 40 and older, with earnings between $20,000 and $500,000. Earnings are projected forward until retirement age, and earnings data are used to estimate the Social Security retirement benefit. Estimates are also made of DB pension benefits for workers who have them, and DC balances. A nominal average return of 6.0% is assumed for financial investments, with a constant rate of increase of 2.8% for the CPI.

The authors estimate optimal saving rates and replacement rates for workers and compare them with estimates of actual saving derived from the SCF. Saving is deemed to be inadequate if the actual savings balance falls short of the model's target by more than 10%. By this yardstick, some 44%

of households are not saving adequately (43% of households in which a male is the "reference person," 49% for females).[49] A particularly striking finding of this paper is that high rates of inadequacy are found for pretty much all demographic groups. For example, even graduate school attendees have a failure rate of 35%, although that is at least lower than the rate of 52% for high school graduates with no college. Households with earnings of $200,000 or more are found to have a failure rate of 43%.

These statistics do not tell us what effort or sacrifice is needed for a household with inadequate savings to get back on track. For a young household for which the optimal balance is low, the extra savings needed during working life might not be large. For older households whose optimal balance is high, the adjustment would be greater. More generally, a given proportional shortfall is likely a more serious matter for a poor household than for a more affluent one.

The Crisis Skeptics

Economists taking a skeptical view of the retirement crisis issue also differ in their approaches, much as the crisis advocates differ in theirs. Hurd and Rohwedder (2011) present and develop a relatively complex model to assess how well-prepared older Americans are for retirement. The very sophisticated model presented in Scholz, Seshadri, and Khitatrakun (2006) is used to address a quite different question—namely, the extent to which Americans nearing retirement have made optimal decisions regarding the amount of their wealth when retirement begins. Brady, Schieber, and Biggs pursue different approaches.

Peter Brady. Peter Brady constructs a model that focuses specifically on the retirement preparedness of wage and salary earners (Brady 2007, 2010, 2016). Brady (2016) relies on data from Social Security and, in particular, on data for six representative workers ages 35 to 44 whose salaries pretty much span the earnings distribution (the lowest paid is at the 18th percentile, the highest is at the 98th).[50] Data on median earnings of the workforce by age

[49]The authors show that retiring earlier will require an increase in saving during working life and will lower the expected replacement rate (asset income and Social Security benefits will be lower). Saving has to increase during working life to even out consumption over the life cycle.

[50]Brady (2016) conducted a study of the regressiveness of 401(k) plans, which considers not just the saving phase but also the decumulation phase, to determine whether benefits are skewed to the better paid. Its conceptual framework is basically the same as the other two studies cited, and the publication (a book published by the Investment Company Institute) is, in the author's view, more accessible than the other two references.

and educational attainment are used to construct six salary profiles.[51] Each representative worker pays both federal and state taxes. (Virginia's tax code is used for this exercise.) No other preretirement income is included other than wages and salaries, and the unit of analysis is the worker, not the household. Consequently, the conclusions are not strictly comparable with most of the other studies discussed in this chapter.

Each worker is assumed to be employed for exactly 35 years, meaning that there are no "zero" years to reduce the Social Security benefit. Income in retirement equals the sum of the Social Security benefit and income from a 401(k) plan earning a real rate of return of 3%, which is assumed to be the only savings instrument. For each of the six representative workers, total savings accumulated by retirement at age 67 is what is necessary to achieve a replacement rate of 94%.[52]

The author does not derive the saving rate from an optimal saving model but rather proposes a pattern of rates for each of the representative workers that he deems to be reasonable. Social Security's progressivity means that the lowest paid worker can start saving later than the better paid and can save at a lower rate. Specifically, the lowest paid worker starts saving at 6% of salary (an employee contribution of 4% and an employer contribution of 2%) at age 52, whereas the worker earning $122,000 starts at age 36, at a rate of 10% including the employer match. Given these assumptions, the replacement rate of 94% is achieved for each group. For income levels between these two points, saving begins at a point between these two ages, with a contribution rate of 9% (see **Table 8**).

In contrast with the other analyses, Brady's analysis can be described as either normative or simply as illustrative. It is not a prediction of the share of US households that will end up with a standard of living equal to that achieved in working life. Instead, it is a conditional calculation of the rate of saving needed given a worker's membership in a 401(k) plan and a consistent record of contributions to that plan to achieve a satisfactory replacement

[51]The six workers' average inflation-indexed annual earnings from age 32 to 66 in 2014 dollars are as follows: $21,000, $43,000, $69,000, $92,000, $122,000, and $234,000. At age 40, the salaries of the second, third, and fourth workers equal the median salaries for workers age 35 to 44 with a high school degree, a bachelor's degree, and a graduate degree. The lowest salary is set equal to one-half of the median earnings of a high school graduate, and the salaries of the two highest earners are a multiple of salary of the worker who earns $92,000. See Brady (2016), p. 11 Figure E.2 footnote 1.

[52]Brady's replacement rate is defined as retirement income net of tax, divided by end-of-career working income net of tax. Most replacement rate calculations use gross income before and after retirement. The figure of 94% comes from another study, and it is an estimate of the net replacement rate that maintains the standard of living achieved during working life in retirement.

Table 8. Starting Age and Saving Rate Necessary to Achieve Targeted Replacement Rate, by Salary

Annual Salary in 2014 dollars	21,000	43,000	69,000	92,000	122,000	234,000
Starting age for saving	52	47	43	37	36	32
Rate of saving (in percent) (combined employer-employee contributions)	6.0	9.0	9.0	9.0	10.0	11.5

Note: Salaries are averages for ages 32–66.

rate. The analysis implies that, if everyone were contributing consistently to a 401(k) plan at a reasonable rate, there would be no crisis. A simple spreadsheet analysis that ignores tax issues would come to the same general conclusion.

Nonetheless, Brady's analysis does point to a basic shortcoming of the current system: its lack of full coverage. With full coverage, a well-designed employee-pension plan should achieve a high degree of retirement security for most workers. As other researchers have emphasized, less than half of the workforce now contributes to an employer-provided plan, although somewhat more than half have access to one. The IRA is available to workers without an employer-provided plan, but its comparatively modest contribution limits would prevent middle-income workers from achieving the deferral rates that might be achieved with a 401(k) plan. (The SEP-IRA, for the self-employed, has much higher contribution limits and one can realistically use this instrument to achieve an acceptable replacement rate.)

Although a worker who is not a member of an employer-provided plan can still save (and a case can be made that younger workers are not being irrational in choosing instead to save for a down payment on a house and then starting to pay off the mortgage), the evidence strongly suggests that workers covered by an employer-provided plan end up with more assets as they approach retirement than workers who have not been covered. Autoenrollment can override inertia, but someone outside a plan can rely only on self-discipline.

Michael Hurd and Susan Rohwedder. Michael Hurd and Susan Rohwedder (2011) develop a rigorously derived empirical model to estimate retirement preparedness for singles and couples who are retired or are nearing retirement. Unlike the NRRI and Rhee's work on the NIRS, Hurd and Rohwedder's model does not attempt to assess the retirement preparedness of younger cohorts. The authors do not follow the approach of comparing estimated or projected replacement rates with targeted rates. They maintain that merely achieving a targeted replacement rate does not guarantee that the standard of living in retirement will be the same as it was when the household was working.

The authors' sample comes from successive waves of the Health and Retirement Study (HRS) at the University of Michigan. The authors derive projections for the path of consumption for each household from an equation whose dependent variable is the *change* in consumption during successive waves for each household in the sample, which is regressed against three categorical variables.

The estimated equation for yearly expenditure changes can be expressed as follows:

$$\frac{c_{t+1} - c_t}{c_t} = \alpha_i + \beta_j + \theta_k + u.$$

The variables α_i, β_j, and θ_k are, respectively, the categorical variables for age, education, and gender. (There are five age categories for singles and four for couples, with the top age category for couples being 80 and older and that for singles being 85 and older, and four categories for education.) Income is not included in the list, although its effect may be captured indirectly by using actual consumption as the baseline value, from which levels of consumption are projected.[53] The estimated values for the categorical variables then can be used to project future consumption for each household.

For most groups, the rate of change is negative, a finding that can be rationalized on the grounds that the increasing probability of death as the household ages encourages the front-loading of consumption. The drop in consumption from one year to the next is greater for singles than for married couples, whose combined longevity will be greater than that of a single person.[54]

The rate of return on assets is an assumed constant. Given projected values for income, derived projections for wealth, and the projected pattern of consumption for each household, as well as survival probabilities derived from the HRS, the authors then determine the probability that a given household can sustain the projected consumption pattern throughout retirement.

[53]The age categories for singles are 65–69, 70–74, 75–79, 80–84, and 85 and older. The education categories are high school incomplete, high school graduate, college incomplete, and college graduate or higher. The coefficients are estimated using median, not ordinary least squares, regression.

[54]Other things equal, the chances of the last to die of a couple who are both 75 living beyond some specific age will be substantially greater than the chances of a single person of the same age reaching that particular milestone.

A household is deemed to be prepared for retirement if the probability of its exhausting its resources before death is no more than 5%.

The study finds big differences in retirement preparedness by gender, marital status, and educational attainment. The preparedness rate for couples is estimated to be 76.8% versus 49.3% for singles. The overall figure is about 71%, which still leaves many households ill-prepared. Interestingly, the preparedness of both singles and married couples with some college but without a degree typically is no greater than that of high school graduates. College students with a completed degree are clearly better prepared, especially if they are married.

The study tested the sensitivity of these results to changes in starting (baseline) consumption. Lowering starting consumption by 10% does increase the proportion of people who are adequately prepared, by 5.2 percentage points among singles and by 3.1 percentage points among couples. These estimates are not a large fraction of the people who are ill-prepared before adopting the consumption reduction, suggesting that some ill-prepared households are definitely "below water." In addition, a clear relationship exists between subjective appraisals of health and preparedness for retirement.

John K. Scholz and Coauthors. Scholz, Seshadri, and Khitatrakun (2006) also develop and apply an elaborate model to investigate the issue of retirement preparedness, but their approach to the issue is in marked contrast to the approaches of the other modelers. They share the skepticism of VanDerhei and Hurd and Rohwedder regarding the usefulness of replacement rates, but they address a different question: rather than trying to gauge the share of Americans who will fail to meet some target replacement rate or be in danger of running out of money before they die, they use their model to determine the extent to which Americans are "optimally" prepared for retirement. The difference is not simply semantic. We are optimally prepared for retirement when our planned pattern of consumption over the future reflects our preferences for consumption now rather than later and can be expected to be financed by our current wealth and expected earnings, if any. Achieving optimality in retirement planning, however, does not guarantee that a future standard of living will be the same as it used to be. That is, an optimal retirement strategy could conceivably involve a reduction in consumption when retiring or at some later time.

The authors construct their model with a sample drawn from participants in the 1992 wave of the HRS who were still alive in 2004. This cohort was born between 1931 and 1941, and their ages in 2004 ranged from 63 to 73. The HRS database includes information on wages and salaries for about 75% of the sample, with the rest being imputed, going back before 1991 so that a record of wages and salaries exists for entire careers. The retired are assumed to live to the age of 100 at most. Their income in retirement is derived from Social Security, DB pensions if they have one or more, and asset income. They face mortality and medical expense risk but not income risk. Working households face earnings risk (earnings are random) but not mortality or medical risk.

For each household, the analysis calculates optimal decision rules. Intuitively, this involves ensuring that the expected marginal utility of consumption, adjusted for the interest rate and the chance of death, is the same for all years.[55] The authors use these rules to calculate optimal consumption (implying optimal wealth) starting with the first year of work given actual earnings in each period. (If actual earnings differ from expected earnings, the pattern of consumption is adjusted.) This operation is repeated for successive years until the age is reached at which actual data on wealth are available for that particular household. The figure thus calculated is that household's optimal wealth, which can be compared with actual wealth.

The paper's main finding is that the share of households with actual wealth below its optimal level is fairly low, at 15.6%. There is not much variation by level of educational attainment. An apparently pronounced relationship between earnings and the share of households with suboptimal wealth is said to reflect the influence of covariates.

The authors conclude that undersaving is more or less randomly distributed through the population. Undersaving, however, is more common with single households, who have lower incomes than married households. The authors calculate that, whether it be the result of low incomes or other influences, 30% of households in the first decile of lifetime earnings have wealth below their optimal target. The share of households that are under water declines steadily. At the fifth decile, it is 16.9%, and at the highest decile, it falls to 5.4%.

The optimizing approach taken by Scholz and coauthors does produce some intriguing results, as noted previously. It does not directly answer the question of how a household's standard of living in retirement compares with the standard achieved during working life.

Using the same basic model and a version of the same dataset used in the earlier paper, the authors address the relationship between optimal saving

[55]The authors use a standard constant relative risk aversion (CRRA) function. For a given period, utility (U) is given by $U = \frac{C^{1-\gamma}}{1-\gamma}$, where γ is the risk aversion parameter. The equation is adjusted to account for the number of children in the family. As explained in Chapter 2, a household with 2 adults and 2 children is equivalent to $(2 + 0.7 \times 2)^{0.7}$, which is the equivalent of 2.4 adults.

and replacement rates (Scholz and Seshadri 2009). Optimal replacement rates are derived from the calculation of optimal saving rates. They calculate the denominator of the replacement rate in two different ways: (1) a measure of lifetime average earnings and (2) an average of income in the ninth- through fifth-to-last years before retirement. The numerator is calculated as the annuitized value of financial and real wealth plus the Social Security benefit and any DB pension income.

Using the first measure as the denominator, they find that the optimal median replacement rate for married people is 0.75, and that for singles is 0.55. They also find substantial variation from one household to the next. For both groups, median replacement rates are lower when the last five years of work are used as the denominator, as might be expected, although the difference between the estimates for the two groups is about the same. The relationship between income levels and educational attainment is less clear cut.

The authors are surely on firm ground in debunking the notion of a single replacement target for all households. They conclude that "while we have not yet solved the problem of what should replace replacement rates, we hope that this work is a first step in a more helpful direction" (Scholz and Seshadri 2009, p. 26). One obvious problem with the authors' approach to optimal saving and a replacement rate that is calculated as part of an optimization exercise is that it is difficult to explain to the noninitiate exactly how optimal replacement rates are derived. It is difficult imagining a financial adviser explaining to a client the rationale for a replacement rate of 0.75, much less 0.55.

An approach that would be in the spirit of Scholz and his coauthors, albeit simpler, would be to begin with an inventory of a client's assets and liabilities, as well as annual income for a series of years. Balance sheet information about households is often overlooked in favor of easier-to-collect income data (Rudd and Siegel 2013). With this information one would include current saving rates, taxes, pending mortgage payoffs, and household size.

Putting this information together should yield an estimate of current expenditure adjusted for any mortgage payoff and changes in expenditure on dependents. At this point, the adviser should be able to determine whether the adjusted expenditure level would be sustainable and, if not, how much of an adjustment would be required. If the current expenditure level is too conservative, the adviser could calculate what a sustainable increase would be. The simplifying assumption is that expenditure is optimal when it can be maintained at a given level. Although this method might seem crude, it nonetheless has the great merit of anchoring the replacement rate calculation on the particular circumstances of each household and would approximate the approach provided by life-cycle theory.

Sylvester Schieber and Andrew Biggs. Two prominent crisis skeptics, Sylvester Schieber and Andrew G. Biggs, have chosen not to develop models as Hurd and Rohwedder and Scholz and Seshadri and their colleagues have done. Instead, they offer critiques of the retirement crisis literature and focus on those parts of the population they regard as most at risk for an insecure retirement.

Work by NIRS has drawn Schieber's and Biggs's fire. In their critique of Rhee (2013), they question the choice of a target replacement rate of 85%. They argue that Rhee's saving assumptions fail to account for the progressive character of Social Security, which means that her estimates of the wealth-to-income ratio needed for a secure retirement are overstated, at least for low-income households. Their own calculations show that low-income workers need not save much to maintain their standard of living in retirement if they worked for at least 35 years (Biggs 2017).

The authors argue that Rhee's assumptions regarding saving are too mechanical and uniform. It would not be unreasonable, for example, to assume that retirement savings would be back-loaded. Young households might focus their savings efforts on a down payment for a home and on rearing children (a kind of investment or at least a necessary expense) rather than on building up the balance of a 401(k) plan. Schieber and Biggs have engaged in debate with other researchers regarding such basic indicators as replacement rates.[56]

Pang and Schieber (2014) completed a survey of most of the issues that arise with efforts to assess retirement preparedness. Many of the points they make have been addressed in this chapter. In particular, the authors address the issue of whether expenditure can be expected to decline as children leave home. Although they acknowledge that the evidence is not entirely clear, the presence of children logically affects expenditure across the entire life cycle. This argument favors accounting for the empty nest effect. Housing wealth also should not be ignored.

The authors acknowledge that being a holder of a supplementary Medicare policy can make most health care risk manageable. They raise the question of whether health care expenditure can be regarded as discretionary.

[56]Biggs and Schieber (2014) responds to a critique by Teresa Ghilarducci of a *Wall Street Journal* op-ed written by Biggs and Schieber. In the latter piece, the authors state that the average US retiree has an income equal to 92% of average American income. Ghilarducci takes issue with this figure, arguing that median retirement income is $16,000 compared with working income of $31,000, implying a much lower replacement rate. Biggs and Schieber argue that the comparison is not valid because the population of retirees is defined in two quite different ways.

If it is discretionary, it can be treated like any other expenditure and has no effect on the replacement rate. If it is necessary, funds ideally should be put aside and excluded from preretirement income (and from the denominator of the replacement rate), as the CRR has done. Another possibility would be to treat some minimum level of expenditure on health care as necessary, while treating the rest as discretionary.

Notwithstanding the authors' apparent admiration for the work on optimal saving, they maintain that a rigorous application of life-cycle theory is not feasible. The calculation and application of replacement rates is a more pragmatic if less theoretically elegant approach.

In Schieber (2015), the author addresses a number of different issues and policy questions related to retirement preparedness. He takes the view that a debate over exactly what percentage of the population is ill-prepared for retirement may not be productive. Instead, he suggests that the efforts of researchers and policy makers might be better devoted to the lot of low-income Americans, because the general consensus is that many of these individuals will enter retirement inadequately prepared. This is a common finding of model simulations, as we have seen. Poorer households are distinguished by their lack of participation in a pension or retirement plan.

The author makes a number of important points. In particular, a mandatory savings program that has only recently been introduced is of little use to those nearing retirement, because they will not have the time to amass a significant amount of additional saving. Imposing such a plan on poorer Americans would be cruel, given that they are already at the poverty line and could end up with income in retirement that exceeded their working-life income. Making the poor pay for a retirement benefit higher than what they currently are earning (net of savings) is not sensible.

The author also addresses the issue of LTC, noting that LTC is an insurance problem, not an inadequate saving problem. As has been discussed, however, LTC can be expensive—at least for those who stay for any length of time in a nursing home or community care arrangement—and long stay patients are a minority. It is not possible to self-insure against LTC unless one is very well off. The insurance problem occurs because the premiums are expensive, crowding out other savings plans, and many applicants do not qualify, for health reasons, for LTC insurance at any price. Finally, the author makes a number of suggestions to broaden the coverage of employer-provided plans.

Taking another tack, Miller and Schieber (2014) have argued that the standard measure of the financial income of older Americans, which comes from the Current Population Survey, is substantially underestimated, particularly for middle- and upper-income Americans. Bee and Mitchell (2017) have explored the issue of underreporting at great depth. Correcting for underreporting mainly due to the underreporting of DB pension income and withdrawals from retirement accounts, and using an extensive array of administrative records, they find that the median income of Americans age 65 and older, which was officially reported to be $33,800, increases to $44,400. The revised estimate of financial income reduces the poverty rate among older Americans from 9.1% to 6.9%. Even if these revisions are accurate, however, they do not necessarily have implications for the financial well-being of future cohorts of retirees.

Biggs (2017) tackles the correct indexation of wage income (broached in Chapter 2). Because the economy-wide average wage tends to grow more rapidly than consumer prices, calculating average income over a long period and using the wage index will result in an average income that is higher than what would be calculated using consumer prices. Hence, the measured replacement rate is lowered.

As Chapter 2 explains, the income level in retirement that is just sufficient to maintain consumption in retirement at the real level attained during working life will be insufficient to permit consumption in retirement comparable to that attainable by those still working, because those still in the workforce benefit from these productivity gains. As such, the replacement rate that is calculated with wage indexation will fall short of the replacement rate calculated with consumer price indexation.

Devotees of wage indexation argue that retired people should benefit from economy-wide increases in productivity, or they will need to benefit from them to compete with working people for scarce resources. In addition, some increases in what have come to be perceived as necessary expenses, like expenditure on cell phones, are not fully reflected in the CPI. Typically, however, economists agree that pension benefits should be indexed to the CPI.

Meir Statman. Meir Statman classifies himself as a skeptic. His view is that there is no *generalized* retirement crisis—that is, one that afflicts a significant share of households at very different income levels. In this respect, his views differ from those of NIRS, for which even a fairly sizable percentage of better-off households are deemed to be headed for a retirement with very short rations.

Statman's analysis is impressionistic, not quantitative. He proposes an approach that recognizes the differing capacities to prepare for retirement of four different economic classes: the wealthy, the steady middle class, the precarious middle class, and the poor. He does not attempt to estimate the size of each of these groups but argues that saving for retirement is a major challenge for two of them—the poor and the precarious middle. The wealthy have incomes high enough that saving is not a challenge.

The steady middle enjoys steady and adequate incomes from the time of their entry into the labor force to their final exit from it—although one wonders what share of the population basks in these happy circumstances—perhaps 15% or 20%—given the decline of both long-term labor market tenure and the role of the DB pension. At any rate Statman assumes that the members of this group are able to save adequately. The poor struggle to keep their heads above water even during their working years, leaving little or no room for retirement saving.

Members of the precarious middle either spend too much or earn too little (or perhaps both). High spenders tend to suffer from lack of self-control and patience. Low earners might have the self-discipline to save, but still find themselves to have inadequate resources at retirement. Financial fragility is widespread among both the precarious middle and the poor. Remarkedly, close to half of the population has reported that, given 30 days to come up with $2,000 for an unexpected expenditure (e.g., money for a car repair), they would not be able to do so without borrowing (Statman 2017, p. 250). A recent survey conducted by the Federal Reserve Board comes to a similar conclusion.

Statman (2017) maintains that standard prescriptions for financial security in retirement are not effective for most of the members of any of the four classes.[57] The wealthy do not need annuities, although a lack of need does not imply that the rich should never buy an annuity, any more than having money to burn makes wasting it a good idea—and the poor simply cannot scrape together the money to buy one. Programs to encourage the poor to save are not effective. A mandatory DC savings plan could help the precarious middle. For the poor, a noncontributory pension may be necessary.

This view may underestimate the potential role that could be played by a mandatory program for the poor. Provided an adequate but not onerous contribution rate could be set that does not entail widespread privation during working life, as Brady has shown, even low-income workers can accumulate enough savings to supplement Social Security adequately.[58]

The 401(k) plans that employers offer, however, are not mandatory. In 2017, about 60% of the employed workforce worked for an employer that offered one of these plans; the take-up rate was about 50% of the workforce at these employers. In Australia, by contrast, about 85% of workers are obliged

[57]Mackenzie (2018) provides a comprehensive review of *Finance for Normal People* (Statman 2017).

[58]See also Sexauer and Siegel (2013).

by their employers to contribute 9.5% of their gross salary. (Unlike the US system, the first tier of the Australian system is means-tested.) In sum, although Statman does not present the kind of dire statistics that the more pessimistic of the crisis advocates do, he does discern a pretty broad social problem.

Surveys of Retirement Confidence

This section summarizes the findings of four recent surveys of retirement confidence. Some of their findings are at odds to some degree with the findings of the crisis advocates, but they do point to some problems, especially among preretirees and in the ability of households to deal with unexpected contingencies.[59]

According to an EBRI 2019 survey (EBRI 2019) of some 2,000 workers and retirees (1,000 each), 67% of workers (age 25 and older) are either very or somewhat confident that they will have enough money to live comfortably during their retirement years. In that respect, however, 33% are either not too confident or not at all confident. As typically is the case with these surveys, retirees are more optimistic about their prospects than workers are. The 2019 survey found that 35% of retirees were very confident of a comfortable retirement and that no less than 82% were either very or somewhat confident, which was up from 75% in 2018 and the highest reading since 1994. The confidence levels of both workers and retirees have rebounded from the lows reached during the Great Recession and have improved since 2018, which probably reflects the buoyancy of the economy in 2018 (the survey was conducted in early 2019).

The confidence edge enjoyed by the retired extends to other financial aspects of retirement. Some 80% of retirees state that they are at least somewhat confident that they will be able to pay for medical expenses, compared with only 59% of workers, although both percentages have increased since 2018. The share of both workers and retirees who express confidence in their ability to meet LTC expenditure drops still further.

The confidence that workers express in being able to enjoy a financially secure retirement notwithstanding, only about one in four workers have tried to calculate how much money they will need to achieve that goal. Moreover, workers tend to overestimate the likelihood of their continuing to work during retirement. In the latest survey, 80% expected to work, but only 28% of current retirees reported that they actually were working. A related phenomenon is a tendency for retirees to stop working earlier than they had planned;

[59]The surveys this study reviews focus on the financial aspects of retirement. For a discussion of a survey of broader issues facing retirees, see Kolluri and Hutchins (2017).

about 43% of respondents retired earlier than planned in 2017, whereas only 9% retired later than planned. The labor force participation rate of older Americans has increased in recent years, but not significantly. Older workers who lose their job typically take longer to find another, and typically those jobs pay less (Simon 2018).

Vanguard. Madamba and Utkus (2017) report on the results of a survey of preretirees and retirees in four countries: the United States, Australia, Canada, and the United Kingdom. A condition for participation in the survey for Americans was having financial assets of at least $50,000. As a result, the average US participant was somewhat more affluent than participants in the EBRI survey.

The qualitative results of the survey were similar to those of the EBRI survey, if somewhat more bullish. In particular, 84% of retirees expressed medium or high satisfaction with their current financial situation, compared with the 79% of preretirees who expected their financial situation in retirement would give them medium or high satisfaction. Some 90% of retirees thought they could at least cover their basic needs. Among preretirees, 83% expected that they would be able to at least cover these needs. Interestingly, 54% of retirees and 59% of preretirees thought that the nation faced a retirement crisis, but only 4% and 10%, respectively, described their situation in those terms. About one in five retirees reported earning wage income in retirement, although as many as 40% of preretirees expected to have wage income once retired.

Transamerica Center for Retirement Studies. A third survey, from the Transamerica Center for Retirement Studies, comes to less sanguine conclusions than the either the EBRI or the Vanguard surveys (Transamerica Center for Retirement Studies 2016). The survey population is defined differently: participants must be at least 50 years of age, must consider themselves to be either semiretired or retired, and must have worked for a for-profit company with 10 or more employees.

Some 72% of the sample expressed that they were somewhat or very confident that they would be able to maintain a comfortable lifestyle in retirement. (Only 46%, however, asserted that they had accumulated a nest egg large enough to finance a comfortable retirement.)

Other questions also elicited some discord with this initial rather optimistic view. Although 90% of survey participants described themselves as generally happy, 28% worried that they would have difficulties making ends meet. About one-third noted that their personal financial situation had deteriorated since retirement, against one-fifth who believed that it had improved. Even more tellingly, 42% cited just getting by as one of their priorities. For one in four retirees, just getting by was in fact their greatest financial priority.

The Transamerica survey confirms the findings of other surveys that there is a marked difference between the median income and savings of married retirees versus that of unmarried ones, which is substantially greater than can be explained by the higher income a couple needs to maintain the same standard of living as a single person. The median savings for married retirees was $224,000 and that for unmarried retirees was $40,000.

The Society of Actuaries. The Society of Actuaries has been conducting comprehensive retirement confidence surveys of both preretirees and retirees for some years. The ninth and latest of these was an online survey (Society of Actuaries 2017) conducted in July 2017 of 2,055 participants between the ages of 45 and 80, pretty evenly divided between 1,030 preretirees and 1,025 retirees.[60] The survey data have been weighted to reflect the basic demographic features of the US population. It is not possible to ensure, however, that the survey's findings are unbiased, given that survey participants self-select.

This survey's findings are on the whole uncontroversial and fairly similar to those of the first three surveys. Both preretirees and retirees worry about being able to maintain a desired lifestyle, and both groups are concerned about the cost of LTC. Both groups also want to be able to "age in place."

The survey does reveal reasons for concern. Only 15% of preretirees consider their accumulated savings to be above target; 33% are on track, but 51% are lagging. Retirees were more likely than preretirees to take protective steps to stay or get back on track: the most common steps included paying off consumer debt and increasing saving by cutting current expenditure. About three-quarters of preretirees *intend* to pay off their mortgages and about one-quarter have already done so. Some 42% of preretirees are planning to claim Social Security at the earliest possible opportunity, lowering the monthly income amount from that source (but lengthening the amount of time they receive it).[61]

[60]Survey participants were classified as retired (1) if that was how they declared themselves; (2) if they had retired from their previous career; or (3) if they were age 65 or older or had a spouse age 65 or older. Anyone not meeting at least one of these tests was deemed to be preretired.

[61]An odd feature of the questionnaire is that saving more and spending less are presented as alternative strategies, when they are the flip sides of the same coin. Unless you can change the amount you earn, you can't save more without spending less. Similarly, the strategy of paying off credit card debt faster than planned requires spending less or the substitution of other presumably less expensive forms of debt.

The survey's findings are not always easy to understand. Some 62% of preretirees and 70% of retirees are confident about their financial situation and can manage their finances, but this appears to reflect confidence in their ability to manage routine current expenditures, such as food, utilities, and rental or mortgage payments, not unexpected costly contingencies. There is concern that such contingencies could upend a retiree's finances.

Many retirees and preretirees are living close to the edge. They also have little awareness of the modalities of LTC financing; in particular, the respective roles played by Medicaid and Medicare are not well understood. (Specifically, both preretirees and retirees tend not to be aware that Medicare does not cover LTC except for a short period. Moreover, as explained earlier, Medicaid's rules are complex and vary from state to state, and they cover only relatively low-priced care, which many retirees would not find adequate.) An additional worry for many is the need to provide for the care of aging parents, a concern that is naturally more common among preretirees and young retirees than it is among older retirees, even if older retirees still find themselves in this situation. The general conclusion the survey suggests is that the inevitable contingencies of retirement and old age are not being properly supported.

The Society of Actuaries also conducted in-depth focus groups to complement its survey program (for a discussion, see Rappaport 2018). Some participants in these groups stress the difference between spending wants and spending needs, suggesting they are able to get by in the face of unexpected shocks to their financial situation by finding ways to make do without some of the expenditure they regularly incurred during their working lives. It is uncertain how widely this sentiment is felt.

4. Does the United States Face a Retirement Crisis? Weighing the Evidence

Retirement security is a pressing issue around the globe. The first three chapters of this study specifically addressed the question of whether the United States either has or is approaching a retirement crisis. (International issues are covered in the final chapter.) As we have discussed, quite apart from the difficulties in finding and interpreting the relevant data, one person's idea of a crisis may simply differ from another. Is it a crisis if 1 in 10 households is expected to fall below some retirement income adequacy benchmark, or should it be at least one in five? What about the size of the average shortfall? Is it a crisis if 1 in 10 households falls below an income level deemed to be adequate with an average shortfall of $1,500 annually, but not a crisis if 1 in 12 falls below that level, with an average annual shortfall of $3,000? How should the likelihood of inadequate income in retirement be weighed against the severity of a shortfall?

We cannot definitively answer these questions, although we should be mindful of an eminent Supreme Court justice's *bon mot*, that although he could not define pornography precisely, he knew it when he saw it. Some numbers, if soundly derived, would imply that a crisis existed by just about anyone's standard. A reliable estimate that 40% of a particular age cohort is headed for a nasty income shortfall in retirement is surely a serious situation, whether or not we call it a "crisis."

This chapter summarizes the main points made in discussing the conceptual issues. That discussion leads to an attempt to establish a benchmark by which different models of financial preparedness may be judged. We then apply this benchmark to each of the models we presented thus far. The chapter closes by setting out tentative conclusions to its analysis of the US situation.

Conceptual Issues

Replacement Rates and Related Issues. The proper definition and measurement of replacement rates raises thorny issues. The first of these issues is the importance of distinguishing between the two different senses of replacement rate: (1) the amount of income in retirement that will provide the same standard of living as was enjoyed in working life, that is, the replacement rate that is desired; and (2) the rate that falls out of an assessment of the resources that are in fact available (expressed as a percentage of the end-of-career income level or some other measure of working-life income). The replacement rate in this second sense is endogenous; it changes when expected wealth at retirement changes, and as other market conditions (such as interest rates) or personal conditions (like life expectancy) change. This second sense is also a target, but it is revised whenever a household's financial circumstances change. The targeted replacement rate is backward looking and is not endogenous. As we have seen, the replacement rate in this second sense will not necessarily equal the targeted rate.

The desired or targeted replacement rate is clearly a useful concept because it forms a goal or benchmark. It is important to know how much income in retirement could take the place of each $1,000 in working income without entailing a decline in the retiree's standard of living. The targeted replacement rate can be used to address a basically factual question: given present trends, will a household's income in retirement be sufficient to maintain its standard of living?

Nonetheless, using the targeted rate raises many issues. One basic issue is the measurement of working income (the denominator of the targeted replacement rate). How many years back should the standard of living assessment go, and how should wages and salaries from earlier years be indexed?

It is not possible to answer the first question objectively. Depending on the path a household's income has taken, it might want to measure working income as an average of many years, or perhaps just a few years at the end of the salary earner's career. When income has been rising steadily for some time, taking the last year probably will overstate the income needed to avoid a decline in the standard of living. Given the difficulty of making an objective choice, researchers and advisers should experiment with the denominator of the replacement rate using various time periods. Both preretiree and retiree income should include the in-kind income from home ownership (and assets should include housing wealth).

It may not be possible to reconcile the contest between wage indexing and consumer price indexing when adjusting for earlier years' wages and salaries in the calculation of the replacement rate's denominator. This debate may reflect differences in social philosophy. Nonetheless, and as this discussion has emphasized, if the goal of retirement policy is simply to maintain the standard of living in retirement that was attained in working life, then CPI indexation should be preferred. Depending on the rate of real growth of wages, moving from wage to price indexation could substantially lower the postretirement income requirement.

The work of John Karl Scholz and his collaborators in particular makes clear that the replacement rate, whether it is the desired (target) rate or a revised target rate, can be expected to vary greatly from one household to the next. It is understandable that a study of retirement readiness with a significant number of participants might use only an average, as in the Aon Hewitt study. It is uncertain whether this approach would bias an estimate of retirement readiness for the whole body of participants, but it certainly would bias the estimates of individual households. Using household-specific replacement rates, if that is possible, is the better choice.

If the data exist, adjustment should be made for the termination of nonrecurrent expenditure streams, like mortgage payments and tuition fees. These expenses are large enough to substantially alter both the target and expected replacement rate. Similarly, changes in household composition, in principle, should have a significant effect on the income needed to maintain the standard of living of those household members who remain.

The evidence on changes in expenditure when children fly the nest is inconclusive. What is not inconclusive is that their departure frees up income (setting aside continuing expenditure such as tuition fees for students in the family). Parents might feel that they've earned a "raise" when the children leave and may be resentful if they cannot spend this income on themselves. It is undeniable, however, that this earned income is not needed to maintain their earlier standard of living.

A good model should take a considered view on the pattern of expenditure after retirement, and in particular, on the substitutability of time for money, while acknowledging that this is a gray area. When the target replacement ratio is allowed to change over the retirement period, the assessment of one's preparedness for retirement can be greatly affected.

Special Risks. A good model must adequately consider the special risks that impinge on the well-being of retirees, including the risk that plans may be upended by job loss or a stock market crash as a household nears retirement (see Chapter 2). Investment and sequence-of-returns risk ideally should be handled stochastically, although assuming a low enough rate of return will reduce the risk of underfunding the retirement. These risks are obviously of greater concern to older Americans relying on asset income. As also noted in Chapter 2, the financial asset holdings of most older Americans, especially holdings of risky assets like stocks and bonds, are modest. A similar issue arises with longevity risk, in that it can be modeled stochastically or can be handled by assuming that a retiree's longevity is sufficiently far above the mean that the probability of surviving to a very old age is low. These analytical shortcuts are little consolation to the retiree who lives to a very old age and runs out of money. Longevity risk needs to be addressed, somehow.

Older Americans who are covered by Medicare and have a supplementary policy—which is most of them—are pretty well protected from the risk of catastrophically costly illnesses. Even so, some older Americans may be vulnerable to high drug costs and possible failures of coverage for particular illnesses. Moreover, the trend in insurance premiums and OOP expenditure is not predictable. In addition, in-home care and the cost of moving to more appropriate housing are rarely if ever insured against, and the retiree needs to budget for these costs.

Medicaid provides a basic safety net for LTC, but the amount of financial protection—the impact of the eligibility rules on an applicant's remaining net worth—can vary significantly from state to state and can be quite inadequate for older Americans at higher income levels. A good planning model should reflect this potential gap in some way. Older Americans who throw themselves on the mercy of Medicaid may find that that the quality of LTC is substandard.

Finally, political risk must be acknowledged. One way of handling this risk would be by a sensitivity analysis, under which different reform scenarios would make differing assumptions about which generation would bear the burden of adjustment. Retired Americans and those nearing retirement probably would be held harmless under most reform proposals, with higher income households being a possible exception. Medicare and Medicaid are also subject to political risk, and the evolution of their costs is far less predictable than the costs of Social Security.

Applying the Benchmark to the Crisis Advocates.

■ *NIRS and Aon Hewitt.* The NIRS studies derive their replacement rate targets from the Aon Hewitt study (Aon Hewitt 2012). The NIRS studies, however, avoid Aon Hewitt's errors regarding the definition of income by instead relying on comprehensive household wealth data from the recent SCF and not just on individual salary incomes.

The NIRS studies derive targets for the wealth-to-income ratio by age of household head from another study (see explanation in Chapter 3). By age 65, the targeted net worth ratio should be high enough to purchase a term-certain 21- or 22-year annuity that generates income at least equal to the target replacement rate. The uniform and rather mechanical adjustment of the net worth targets by age may lead to an overstatement of the retirement shortfall when households are young if retirement saving tends to be backloaded. If this is the case, the targets really should be lower at younger ages. Finally, these studies offer no explicit treatment of medical cost and LTC cost risk.

The Aon Hewitt study (Aon Hewitt 2012), then, is seriously flawed. Its estimates of the degree of preparedness of preretirees for retirement (or the lack thereof) may be right, but if so, they are right for the wrong reasons.[62] The study's flaws stem from its choice of the individual rather than the household as the unit of analysis. The measure of income of the individual employees who are the object of its analysis is not comprehensive, and the income of other members of the household is ignored. Ignoring the income from other sources of plan participants, as well as the income and retirement income of other family members, would have an uncertain but potentially highly distorting effect on the expected replacement ratio.

The Aon Hewitt study handles longevity risk by assuming that retirees live somewhat longer than their life expectancy. This may well be what a reasonably prudent retiree would do, although it leaves unusually long-lived retirees at risk at a time when they can't do much about it. The rate of return on investments is assumed to be constant, although some sensitivity analysis is conducted. Medical and LTC costs are not analyzed stochastically but a limited range of alternative assumptions is explored, and political risk is not analyzed. The shortcomings of this study and its subsequent updates are not redeemed by their large sample size.

■ *Center for Retirement Research, EBRI, Warshawsky.* The work of the Center for Retirement Research at Boston College and EBRI is light-years ahead of the simpler approaches just discussed, as is that of Mark Warshawsky and his collaborators. The treatment of housing equity by the CRR's National Retirement Risk Index considers the in-kind income from home ownership. The NRRI's treatment of longevity risk allows it to derive estimated replacement rates, household by household, by assuming that all financial assets are annuitized. This is one way of dealing with the longevity risk issue, at least in a theoretical model, but it does not deal with longevity risk in practice. Setting aside low-income Americans reliant entirely or mostly on Social Security, most assets are *not* annuitized.

An important implication of the CRR's model is that a household that is within 10% of its target replacement rate (or above the target) cannot run out of money. In practice, however, it could, for several reasons, including unexpected expenses and living above one's means. Yet another reason, which we'll focus on more closely, is deviation of actual longevity from expected longevity.

[62]Updates of the 2012 study (Aon Hewitt 2015 and 2018) arrive at broadly similar conclusions. They do not provide the same detailed discussion of underlying assumptions and analytical methods, although they are described as "full" reports. The 2018 report includes interesting discussions of retirement readiness by generation and gender.

Suppose that 60% of households are on track, and 40% are not on track, for an adequate retirement income. Suppose further that 25% of on-track households (15% of all households) would in practice fall short because they live beyond their life expectancy, and 25% of off-track households (10% of all households) are in fact on track because they die before reaching life expectancy. The adjusted numbers in such a case would be 55% of all households on track and 45% off track. The CRR's approach is correct if we assume that households all have actual longevity equal to that which was expected, or if all retirement income was in fact annuitized.

Notwithstanding the sophistication of the work of the CRR and that of Mark Warshawsky and his collaborators, EBRI's model is the gold standard of retirement risk modeling. It takes explicit account of investment and sequence-of-returns risk, and because it does not annuitize all assets at retirement, it then can track the relationship between longevity and the risk of running out of money. Its painstaking modeling of 401(k) contributions allows it to undertake policy simulation exercises of changes to the rules governing these plans. Inevitably, these valuable features come at the cost of extra complexity. The treatment of consumption expenditure in retirement by both EBRI and Warshawsky does raise some issues, as we have noted. Warshawsky's approach can tell us whether a shortfall is likely, but not what the depth of the shortfall will be—although the model probably could be adapted to achieve that end. EBRI's model does both.

The Crisis Skeptics. Schieber, Biggs, and Statman would all agree that low-income households preparing for retirement are at greater risk of a distressing decline in their standard of living than other households. Their approach, however, is not as comprehensive in its scope as that of most other researchers, although the first two researchers do successfully poke holes in the arguments of the more dire prognosticators.

The rigorous modeling approach of Hurd and Rohwedder leads to a more sanguine conclusion than those of EBRI or the CRR. The difference between these approaches may be explained by differences in their treatment of the basic risks retirees face and the way they determine targeted or normal consumption expenditure in retirement. Brady advances what he calls illustrative, but what might be better called normative, arguments that penury in retirement can be avoided with a program of sustained contributions to a DC plan at an adequate rate.

The approaches taken by Scholz and colleagues and Warshawsky and colleagues are somewhat similar, but they lead to different conclusions. Notably, their conclusion—that most Americans are saving "optimally" for retirement—does not imply that these retirees will achieve a standard of living in retirement approximating what they enjoyed while working. To think otherwise is to commit a logical error. An optimal decision is the best one that can be made in the current state of the world. An embattled military commander may be making the best decisions available in the fog of war, but that does not guarantee victory. So this use of the word "optimal" does not conform to the way the word often is used in ordinary speech, which is that everything will turn out for the best.

Estimates of the percentage of older Americans making optimal decisions might be close, however, to the percentage maintaining their preretirement incomes in retirement in a relatively stable economic and financial environment. The closeness of the two percentages also would be affected by the degree of aversion to variations in the standard of living over time and the rate at which future income is discounted.

The work by John Karl Scholz and his coauthors is important for another reason: it implies that the great majority of the members of at least one cohort of retirees were not prone to shortsightedness or faulty financial decision making as they prepared for retirement. That certainly is heartening news, although it is not consistent with much of what has been written about financial literacy and decision making.

Behavior of Wealth-to-Income Ratios. Before summing up, we take another look, as promised, at the SCF's figures for the ratios of net worth to income for older US households. The behavior of net worth ratios suggests that however ill- or well-prepared for retirement older US households were in 1989, the degree of their preparedness may have held steady or even improved over the 1989–2016 interval. Because the stock market has continued to rise since 2016, this conclusion probably still applies today.

It is unlikely, however, that a given wealth-to-income ratio in 1989 would support the same standard of living in 2016 or later. Munnell et al. (2014) give five reasons why contemporary wealth-to-income ratios need to be increased to maintain the same standard of living enjoyed by retirees 25 years ago:

- Increases in the full retirement age (FRA) reduce Social Security's replacement rate over time—for example, if the replacement rate from Social Security alone was 40% at age 65, and the Social Security benefit was reduced by 5%, the replacement from Social Security alone drops by 2 percentage points.
- The move from DB to DC pensions should increase measured wealth (but not actual wealth, including the present value of expected DB plan benefits) if workers compensate for declining participation in DB plans by

contributing commensurately more to DC plans. Looking at DC plans alone will overstate pension wealth, because measures of pension wealth typically exclude the wealth represented by interests in a DB plan.

- Rising health care costs, which particularly affect older Americans, may mean that a CPI geared for older Americans has increased at a significantly faster rate than the regular CPI.
- Increasing life expectancy, which affects the annuity income generated by financial assets, or the portion of asset value that can be consumed if annuities are not purchased; it does not directly affect SS benefits or income from the conventional DB pension.
- Real interest rates have declined substantially and are now negative at the shorter end (e.g., for five-year maturities as of January 2020).

We consider each of these influences in turn.

The normal age (i.e., the FRA) for the full Social Security retirement benefit was for many years set at 65. It began to change for cohorts born in 1938 or later, reaching 66 for cohorts born between 1943 and 1954. Retirees in 1995 age 62 and born in 1933 thus would be taking retirement three years before the FRA, which still would be 65 years. People retiring in 2016 at age 62 would be taking retirement four years before the FRA that applied to their cohort. The extra year of early retirement would reduce their pension by 5%. This calculation assumes that the change in the FRA has no effect on the timing of a claim. Other things equal, this benefit reduction would require an offsetting increase in net assets or an additional period of work.

A huge swing in the number of active participants from DB plans to DC plans (mainly 401(k) plans) has taken place in the private sector over the past 25 years. Between 1989 and 2014, the number of active participants in the private sector DB plans fell from 27.1 million to 14.5 million, whereas the number of active participants in DC plans increased from 33.9 million to 75.4 million, as reported by the Employee Benefits Security Administration (EBSA 2016). The number of formerly active DB plan participants receiving pensions, however, is estimated to have increased from 12.8 million to 23.3 million over this period. This substantial increase reflects the strong growth in active plan participation 25 to 30 years earlier. The difficulty entailed by the interpretation of this data makes the role of the declining importance of the DB pension on retirees' standards of living hard to discern.

OOP medical expenses include insurance premiums, copays, coinsurance, and uncovered expenses. Some components of the OOP costs of older Americans have been increasing rapidly, most notably Medicare Part B premiums. These increases have been tempered somewhat by the introduction of the Medicare drug benefit (Part D), and the subsequent start of the closing of the "donut hole," a feature of the original legislation that left beneficiaries uncovered over a certain range of expense. A recent study by McInerney, Rutledge, and King (2017), using data from the Health and Retirement Study, finds that OOP spending dollars declined by 9% between 2004 and 2014 (expressed in constant 2014 dollars), or from an average of $4,700 to $4,274. As a result, the share of Social Security benefits spent on these costs declined. The study concludes, however, that the share of Social Security benefits devoted to medical expenditure leaves only limited income for non-medical expenditure for many elderly people.

The increase in longevity means that more wealth is required to sustain the same level of income over time. We assume that the increased longevity can be captured by the increase in life expectancy between 1990 and 2015 for 65-year-old men. The Social Security's actuaries estimated that remaining life expectancy increased from 19.4 to 21.5 years over this period. Assuming a real discount rate of 3%, the value of a constant annual income stream would increase by 7.8%. The financial assets needed to generate the longer income stream would have to increase accordingly.

The impact of declining interest rates, even if we know the total value of someone's financial assets, is difficult to gauge, because it will depend on the particular characteristics of the financial assets held. We assume that a household holds financial assets that make equal annual payments over 15 years at a rate of interest equal to that of the 10-year Treasury bond. In 1989, the real rate on Treasuries was 4.5%; as of early 2020, it was about zero. A $50,000 investment at the 1989 rate could finance annual income of $4,656 for 15 years; at the much lower interest rate currently prevailing, the income would have declined by almost 25% to $3,333.[63] The potential for large capital losses is also a concern. Declining interest rates and increasing longevity combine to lower the amount of sustainable income from a given amount of wealth. This effect could be substantial.

The additional saving needed to offset these various influences depends on the composition of a retiree's income. As noted, a remarkably large number of older Americans have little or no investment income. The median share of investment income in the total income of households headed by 65–74-year-olds is zero, according to the SCF for 2016; in three of four of

[63]A further complication is the potential for capital gains or losses on instruments with long maturities, although if the gains were realized, the proceeds still would have to be reinvested at lower interest rates. Yet another issue is the behavior of stock prices, because a substantial share of the financial assets of older Americans is held in equities.

these households, investment income is less than 1% of total income. In the case of households headed by 75-year-olds or older, in three of four of these households investment income is less than 2% of the total. The share of investment income does rise with income, but even for those households in the top decile of income, its median value remains moderate. For households in this decile headed by 65–74-year-olds for example, the median value is 5%. For households with heads age 75+, the median value is 23%.

The share of financial assets taking the form of direct or indirect holdings of equities rises rapidly with income. In the top decile, the median share of equities in households' financial assets was 49% in 2016. To sum up, it is hard to draw definite conclusions about the impact of the decline in interest rates on the wealth needed to sustain a given income stream, especially given the sometimes-offsetting swings in equity and bond prices.

Given the composition of retirement wealth for older Americans in the lowest two income deciles, the major effect on the wealth needed to maintain a given expenditure level for these households results from the changes to Social Security's normal retirement age. This effect, in principle, can be offset by delaying claiming by a single year—for example, from age 62 to age 63 (or age 63 to age 64) and instead working that additional year. If retirees could afford not to work for an extra year, they would begin retirement with a lower level of income. For many, this would not be either a feasible or desirable strategy; for others, it might be.

Note, however, that the extra year of work required to achieve the same Social Security benefit would allow the retiree to bank at least some of the extra year's disposable income. These considerations suggest that the wealth-to-income ratios needed to maintain a given sustainable replacement rate have risen over the past quarter century and that preparedness for retirement has deteriorated at any given wealth-to-income ratio, but that the extent of the deterioration will vary substantially with individual circumstances.

Is There a Retirement Crisis? We return to our basic question as it pertains to the United States: is there a retirement crisis, or not? The most sophisticated models imply that anywhere from 25% to 50% of US households preparing for retirement will end up short of the savings they will need. In the CRR's current scenario, about one in two households will end up at least 10% under water. EBRI projects that a significant share of households will run out of money without major changes to the 401(k) system, although the size of the shortfall may not always be large. Warshawsky's work reaches a similar conclusion. Hurd and Rohwedder are the most optimistic, but even their model projects an ill-preparedness rate of about 25%. The surveys of retirement readiness we have summarized support this conclusion on the whole, although these surveys are not always easy to interpret. The one finding that really stands out is the apparent unpreparedness of older Americans for the unexpected.

To be sure, many issues are unresolved, and these issues can work in either direction. The issue of whether expenditure can decline as we age without jeopardizing our welfare is not entirely resolved, nor is the impact of changing family size and (to a lesser extent) nonrecurrent expenditure. The fact that the wealth-to-income ratios were well below the calculated ratios needed to sustain an income level close to preretirement income in 1989 is something of a puzzle—we do not see a large population of impoverished elderly. This population likely made adjustments not accounted for by the standard financial models, such as moving in with their children, relocating to lower-cost areas, and working longer.

The biggest unresolved issues, however, are the impending adjustment that must sooner or later be made to Social Security and the uncertain state of the finances of Medicare and Medicaid. This needed adjustment to Social Security alone will jeopardize the retirement security of many Americans or oblige them to reduce their current standard of living to prevent an undue fall in that standard when they retire. Crisis or no crisis, many US households still some ways from retirement have a good deal to be anxious about.

Chapter 3 provided a detailed review of a large number of quantitative studies of retirement security in the United States. This review could not be conducted for the non-US countries reviewed in Chapter 5, but a preview of that chapter with general observations still can be made here. In the large countries of continental Europe, the major issue is the sustainability of the current system in light of growing pressure on public finances in each country. In Canada, the first pillar of the retirement system does not confront the same pressures as the US system, but the coverage of private pensions certainly could be broader. In the United Kingdom, the private component needs to play a bigger role, and in Australia, the major issue may be the workings of the distributive phase of the system.

As for health, the United States faces a generalized problem with the provision and financing of health care—specifically, the less-than-universal coverage of Americans before reaching age 65, and the poor value for the money of the system as a whole. Health care coverage in the non-US G–7 countries and in Australia is discussed in Chapter 5.

5. Comparison of Pensions and Health and Long-Term Care Costs Across Countries

This chapter compares and contrasts the major institutional features of pension systems and health care in the United States with those of the other G–7 countries (the G–6) and Australia. The data presented here amount to a series of aggregate snapshots of various aspects of the current adequacy and coverage of the countries' pension and health systems. Although this chapter does not include the kind of detailed information that was provided in Chapter 3, one can glean some ideas of the sustainability of these other countries' average benefits and their treatment of low-income households from the structure of their systems and related data. Even a broad-brush analysis of such major structural features as the relative role of public and private pensions and the role of private financing in health care allows us to say something about the basic risks that retirees face in the major industrial countries.

General Considerations

Almost all countries with pension systems, and especially the systems of industrial countries, have been affected by the declining birth rates and rising life expectancies that took place in the wake of World War II. These trends are expected to continue (OECD 2019a).

The impact of population aging is most obvious with pay-as-you-go DB public pension systems, in which the current pension payments are paid for by the contributions of current workers. Declining birth rates and increasing life expectancy increase the old-age dependency ratio—that is, the ratio of the number of retired people to the number of workers—requiring either an increase in payroll taxation to finance a given pension, or a decline in pension benefits, or some combination of the two. Among the large industrial countries, the old-age dependency ratio is highest in Japan and Italy.

DC systems, however, are vulnerable to the same effect. A declining or more slowly growing workforce means that the same capital stock is less productive. More saving is then required to finance the increase in physical, technological, or human capital needed to maintain the incomes of workers and the retired. Rising life expectancy means that the claims of the elderly on the national income increase, again requiring an increase in saving and capital accumulation to prevent declines in living standards. Declining birth rates and increasing longevity affect pension systems regardless of the financial arrangements of the systems.[64]

Basic Structural Features of Pensions in Countries with Systems Similar to the United States

Australia, Canada, and the United Kingdom have pension systems that resemble that of the United States, as befits (in the case of the United States, Canada, and Australia) their history as former English-speaking colonies with a common law background.[65] The systems of the United Kingdom and Canada, especially the latter, are the most similar to that of the United States, whereas Australia is in some respects an outlier, being the only country in the group where employer-provided pensions are mandatory, and where the public component mostly takes the form of a DC plan. This exposition will focus on these three countries, while making some observations about the pension systems of the larger industrial countries that make up the rest of the G–7, which are less similar.[66]

Canada. Canada's system, with respect to both its public and private components, is the most similar to the US system. The Canada Pension/Quebec Pension Plan (CPP/QPP) is financed by a payroll tax on employers and employees and pays a DB pension that is related to the number of years worked and salary.[67] Employer-provided plans are not mandatory

[64]See Mackenzie (2006), Appendix 2, for further discussion.

[65]Mackenzie (2010) includes an appendix with profiles (vignettes) of 10 industrial countries, including Australia, Canada, the United Kingdom, and the United States, as well as Germany, Japan, Switzerland, Denmark, the Netherlands, and Sweden. It is somewhat dated but does provide useful discussions of historical developments and basic institutions. The treatment of each country also includes a brief discussion of issues pertaining to financial literacy and the consequences of the Great Recession. New Zealand, with its very small population, is not covered here, although it does have some features in common with the other four countries. Turner and Rajnes (2016) is a more current reference. Abbott et al. (2009) is a collection of papers on more specialized aspects of Canada's system.

[66]The employer-provided component of the French system is effectively a part of the public component. It is a DB system financed by payroll tax rates set by the government.

[67]The rate of tax on employer and employee is 4.95% (5.95% under the QPP) and is scheduled to rise in steps to 5.95% by 2025. The self-employed pay both halves, as in the United States. The maximum earnings level on which taxes are levied is C$54,900, which is substantially less than its US counterpart. It is scheduled to rise (in 2016 dollars to C$82,700 by 2025). The minimum retirement age is 60 years old, two years lower than in the United States. Unlike the US system, the replacement rate is constant and does not decline with income. It is scheduled to increase from 25% to 33% for low- to middle-income earners, with a lower increase for higher-income earners, so the replacement rate will not be constant across incomes after that change. Canada has a social assistance component to its system, the Old-Age Supplement

and most provincial jurisdictions do not require autoenrollment. As in the United States, the federal government encourages voluntary saving for retirement through tax-favored schemes, both employer-provided and individual. Taxation in Canada, like most countries, applies the "exempt, exempt, taxed (EET)" rule, with contributions and capital accumulation being exempt and distributions being taxed. In the United States, that rule applies to 401(k) plans and to the traditional IRA. Roth IRAs are taxed at the contribution stage and are exempt at the accumulation and distribution stages.

In Canada, the coverage rate of the personal component of private sector schemes is similar to that of the occupational component (see **Table 9**), reflecting the basically voluntary character of the personal component. Among the major industrial countries, Germany has broader coverage by employer than either Canada or the United States, although employer-provided pensions in Germany are not as large on average as those of these two countries. Both Canada and the United States have suffered a marked decline in the role of the traditional DB pension in the past 20 to 30 years, although its

Table 9. Coverage of Funded and Private Pension Plans, Latest Year Available (in percent of the working-age population, 15 to 64 years)

	Mandatory/ Quasi-Mandatory	Auto-Enrollment	Voluntary		
			Occupational	Personal	Total
Australia	75.2	x	x	...	...
Canada	x	...	26.4	24.9	...
France	x	x	25.2	7.8	...
Germany	x	...	57.0	33.8	70.4
Italy	x	...	10.1	12.3	20.6
Japan	...	x	50.5	14.7	54.3
United Kingdom	x	46.0	...	5.0	...
United States	x	...	43.6	19.3	...

Note: x = Not applicable; ... = not available. Coverage rates are provided with respect to the total working-age population (i.e., individuals ages 15 to 64 years old), except for Germany (employees ages 25 to 64 subject to social insurance contributions). Data refer to 2018 or to the latest year available.
Source: OECD (2019a).

(OAS), which depends not on earnings but on the number of years of residence in the country. It also has a disability component. See Social Security Administration (2017) for a fuller description of the Canadian system.

predominance in the Canadian public sector, which is proportionately larger than its US counterpart, has to some extent moderated the decline in that country (Mackenzie 2010).

The OECD reports that average replacement rates in Canada and the United States provided by both components for full career workers who began work in 2016 and who are expected to work a full career are similar (see **Table 10**) and are among the top three of the G–7 plus Australia.

Unlike the US system, the CPP (but not the QPP) is partially funded. The chief actuary makes projections out 75 years, which are revisited every three years. Given current levels of mortality, it is not expected to require additional funding. Investments are managed by a politically independent investment board. If the chief actuary determines after a review that additional funding is required, legislation requires an automatic adjustment. In these respects, the CPP, if not the QPP, differs from its US counterpart.

The most striking differences between Canada and the US pertain to the regulatory framework that applies to the public component and to the way the public component's reserves are invested. The CPP's reserves are invested in the financial markets and overseen by a board subject to an elaborate regulatory framework designed to ensure competent and disinterested management. Reforms along these lines have been proposed for the Social Security Trust Fund but have never gained much traction.

United Kingdom. The UK system has been subject to a series of reforms over the years, with the result that differing regimes apply to different vintages of workers and pensioners. The version that applies to workers who

Table 10. Gross and Net Pension Replacement Rates for Mandatory Public and Private and Voluntary Pension Schemes (in percent of individual earnings)

	Mandatory Public and Private	Voluntary	Total
Australia	30.9	. . .	30.9
Canada	39.0	25.1	64.1
France	60.1	. . .	60.1
Germany	38.7	13.5	52.2
Italy	79.5	. . .	79.5
Japan	32.0	23.8	55.8
United Kingdom	21.7	29.1	50.9
United States	39.4	29.7	69.1

Note: The calculations are for full-career workers earning their country's average wage.

retire at age 65 for men and 63 for women on or after April 6, 2016, is a single-tier state pension (STP), which is a flat rate pension whose benefit depends on the number of years worked, not earnings. A full benefit is earned after 35 years of work. A precipitous decline has taken place in the relative role of DB pensions in the United Kingdom (Mackenzie 2010). Coverage of the private component is lower, as is the average replacement rate, especially for the public component (see Tables 9 and 10), in part because the STP does not increase with earnings.

A relatively recent innovation, the National Employment Savings Trust (NEST) was introduced in the United Kingdom as a part of a number of reforms implemented in 2008 that included the introduction of autoenrollment. The NEST is a multiemployer DC pension scheme open to any employer that chooses to participate in it. The self-employed, amounting to about 14% of the workforce, are excluded, however, and about one-fifth of the employed labor force is ineligible for the program because they do not meet its age or earnings requirements (OECD 2018, p. 23).

Australia. The Australian system bears certain similarities to that of the United States, in particular, the dominant role now played there by DC plans, which is even greater than the role DC plans play in the United States. This simply reflects the fact that employers are required to enroll all their full-time and many of their part-time workers in the Superannuation (Super for short) system, with an across-the-board contribution rate that is now 9.5, but that is to be increased to 10% in 2021 and to 12% in 2025. As a result, the Super's coverage of the active labor force reaches 85%. Funds can be either industry based—that is, offered to workers in a particular industry—or retail accounts, and choices are subject to a default setting.

There is, however, a crucial difference between the two countries: in Australia, the first tier, which is known as the Age Pension, is means-tested and contributes little to the replacement rates of the better paid. The regulatory function is in the hands of a single agency, the Australian Prudential and Regulatory Agency or APRA. This concentration of regulatory authority may be more feasible in Australia because of the much smaller population of the country.

The Age Pension is subject to both an asset test and an income test (Australian Government 2020). Candidates must pass both tests to receive it, and the pension benefit is determined by a sliding scale applying to both assets and income. As an example pertaining to the income test, for a single person age 66—the current qualifying age—who is not disabled, with annual income from all sources including retirement income less than roughly

$3,100 per year, the annual Age Pension benefit is about $17,000.[68] The pension is reduced by 50% of any income above that amount and dwindles to zero once income is about $37,200 or higher. For a couple living together with a combined annual income of about $5,600 or less, the pension will be about $25,700. The Age Pension drops to zero at a combined income of about $57,000. In other words, for both retired single people and couples with income from the Super and other sources (including wages and salaries, if the single person or one or both members of the couple are still working), the first pillar simply disappears at a moderate income level.

Lump sums may be drawn from one's Super fund balance—it is not necessary to take it as a flow of income—and lump-sum withdrawals reduce the value of the income subject to the income test (although if not spent, the withdrawal counts toward the asset test). This provision reduces the incentive to annuitize at least of part of the balance in a Super account and encourages spending. Recently, the government has taken measures that encourage the annuitization of retirement income (OECD 2019a).

In the United States, Social Security plays an important role in contributing to a decent replacement rate for retired middle-income households that have substantial income from their holdings of 401(k) plans, IRAs, or other sources. Middle-income workers in Australia do not benefit from the same degree of support from the first tier. In addition, the income that the Super generates typically is not in the form of an annuity. The sliding-scale nature of the Age Pension and the lack of annuitization are problematic features of the Australian system. Considerations like these may lie behind the recent legislation to raise the contribution rate, although contribution rate increases do not address the annuitization issue directly.

The unorthodox design of the Age Pension contributes to the relatively low ratio of the average income of older people to that of the Australian population as a whole. A similar difference exists in the United States and the United Kingdom, but it is not nearly as large (see **Table 11**). The low ratio results in part from the phase out of the Age Pension already noted. The equivalent rule in the United States might mean that, say, any older person with all other income sources adding to about $45,000 would no longer receive a monthly check of any amount from Social Security. The Age Pension does help workers whose incomes have always been very low, however. Poverty rates increase with the age of the elderly and are higher among women than men.

[68]This figure includes certain supplementary payments. The text's values are expressed in US dollars, at an exchange rate of 1 US dollar being equal to 1.42 Australian dollars, the rate prevailing on December 31, 2019.

Table 11. Incomes of Older People, 2016 or Latest Available Year (average income in percent of average income of total population)

	All Ages Over 65	Age 66–75	Age Over 75
Australia	72.3	77.9	63.9
Canada	90.5	94.1	84.9
France	103.2	107.6	97.7
Germany	88.6	92.5	85.1
Italy	99.6	107.8	91.4
Japan	87.8	89.7	85.5
United Kingdom	83.6	90.6	73.9
United States	93.8	102.1	80.9

Source: OECD (2019a).

The voluntary character of participation in US employer-provided plans means that many US workers will retire without significant retirement plan assets if they either (1) did not have such a plan available to them or (2) chose not to participate or to take advantage of an employer contribution match. Even if they participated but made only small contributions, they will have a low income in retirement. This is not the case in Australia because of the Super's mandatory character.

A recent report from the Australian government's Productivity Commission is quite critical of certain aspects of the system, including the unnecessary and unintended multiple accounts that result when a worker changes jobs—this is also an issue in the United States—as well as what the report terms "entrenched underperformers" (Australian Government 2018). Underperformance is more of a problem with retail funds than it is for industry funds. (Workers are not bound to enroll in their industry funds.) The report also finds abundant evidence of excessive and unwarranted fees. The government is not required to act on the many recommendations the report makes to deal with these issues, but it appears that it is giving the report's findings serious consideration.

One important difference between the public component of the pension system in the United States and those of the other three countries is that Australia, Canada, and the United Kingdom offer some combination of a basic pension (either contributory or noncontributory), a minimum pension, and targeted social assistance. The United States does provide social assistance in the form of the SSI, but Social Security is not subject to a minimum and there is no basic pension. Retirees have to work for at least 40 quarters to obtain a benefit of any amount from Social Security—otherwise, they receive the SSI payment, which is small, as a substitute.

The United Kingdom has a basic pension that does not depend on income, but it does not have a minimum pension or social assistance. Canada has a minimum pension and provides social assistance, and Australia has the means-tested Age Pension (see **Table 12**). The coverage of targeted social assistance is by far the highest in Australia because of the large share of older people receiving an Age Pension, even if the amount received can be modest.

On the basis of these macro-indicators in the other countries with systems similar to that of the United States, and the remaining G–7 countries (France, Germany, Italy, and Japan), we would hazard an assessment of the vulnerability of their elderly population to the risks identified in Chapter 2, leaving a discussion of health care and LTC cost risk to the comparative section on health issues later in this chapter. With respect to longevity risk, Australia stands out as a poor provider of hedges against this risk. The Age Pension does provide some insurance against longevity risk, but its role fades as other income increases in importance.

The balances accumulated in the Super could be invested at least partly by the retiree in commercial annuities. Australians, like Americans, have never

Table 12. Current Level and Recipients of First-Tier Benefits

	Benefit Value in 2018 (% of AW earnings)				Recipients in 2016 (% of population age 65 and older)			
	Residence-Based Basic	Targeted	Contribution-Based Basic	Minimum	Residence-Based Basic	Targeted	Contribution-Based Basic	Minimum
Australia		27.8				69		
Canada	13.3	16.8			97	31		
France		25.4		22.3		4		39
Germany		20.0				1		
Italy		18.8		21.1		7		32
Japan		18.4	15.0			3	91	
United Kingdom		21.6	16.7			19	107	
United States		16.4				2		

Note: The benefit level shown is for new pensioners in 2018. Recipient data for Italy are from 2012.

been enthusiastic about such annuities, however, and they usually take disbursements as lump sums. Whatever its other merits, the Super provides less longevity risk protection than the public systems of any of the other countries, except perhaps for low-income earners. The French and Italian systems provide the most longevity insurance because of the large share of retirement income that the indexed annuity in those countries provides.

With respect to investment risk, Australia also stands out because of the dominant role played by the Super, the only mandatory DC plan among the eight countries. The Super is a DC plan, and investment risk is entirely borne by the participants. They may choose to invest their assets conservatively, but OECD data show that the share invested in equities is relatively high. That share is also fairly high in the voluntary plans of the United States, but the share is somewhat lower in Canada and lower still in the United Kingdom (see **Table 13**). It is clearly low in the large continental countries.

In Australia, the scheduled increases in the Super's contribution rate will mitigate the consequences of investment risk, but it will not reduce investment risk itself. Because the asset allocation is at the participant's discretion, an adequate degree of financial literacy is especially important in those countries where the role of DC plans (like the 401(k) and IRA in the United States and the Super in Australia) is significant.

Political risk is lower in Australia than it is in the other countries. This is the big advantage of Australia's choice of a compulsory, public DC system. The government is not promising its current or future pensioners a

Table 13. Allocation of Assets in Funded and Private Pension Plans in Selected Asset Classes and Investment Vehicles, 2018 or Latest Year Available (in percent of total investment)

	Equities	Bills and Bonds	Cash and Deposits	CIS (when no look-through)	Other
Australia	43.7	14.6	13.7	...	28.1
France	38.1	22.4	34.5	...	5.0
United States	30.7	24.5	2.5	31.6	10.6
Canada	28.7	31.7	4.0	...	35.6
Italy	18.2	45.1	6.3	...	30.4
United Kingdom	9.0	30.2	2.2	26.6	31.9
Japan	8.1	31.6	8.7	...	51.6
Germany	5.4	49.9	4.2	...	40.6

Note: CIS = collective investment schemes.
Source: OECD (2019a).

pension like the US Social Security payout or the pensions of the other G–7 countries—just the Age Pension, the cost of which is not onerous. In other words, the Age Pension aside, the government's own balance sheet is not being used to guarantee the benefit. That said, a failure of the current system to provide adequate retirement income because of poor performance of the Super could put pressure on the government to take compensatory measures. Political risk is a serious issue in the large continental countries because of the outsize role played by public pensions in providing retirement security in those countries and also because of the large share of pension expenditure in total public expenditure.

Financial Developments in Health and Long-Term Care in Other Countries Compared with the United States

The economics and financial aspects of health care (effectively medical care) are remarkably complex, although fascinating.[69] This section focuses on the financing of health care and LTC in the same countries covered in the pensions section and briefly addresses the related topic of access to health care. It will again draw largely on work of the OECD. Because the costs of health care should *in principle* be related to its quality and coverage, this section briefly discusses some standard indicators of the quality of health care in the countries covered as well as micro-indicators of quality and access.

The OECD estimates that, in 2016, health care expenditure in the United States amounted to more than $10,000 per capita and thus to almost 17% of GDP. In Germany, the next highest spender, the comparable figure is just under $6,000 (see **Table 14** and **Table 15**).[70] Growth rates of health expenditure have moderated in recent years both in the United States and elsewhere, but their rate of growth remains above general inflation.

[69]Peter Diamond, the Nobel Prize winner and coinventor of the overlapping generations model of pension economics, is supposed to have said something to the effect that the economics of Social Security and pensions was child's play compared with health.

[70]When the incomes or expenditures of different countries are compared on a purchasing power basis as they are in Table 14, incomes are typically converted to US dollars at a recent nominal exchange rate, but then are adjusted for differences in the cost of living or the cost of the services being compared. For example, if the average food budget in some other country was one-third that of a US household taking account only of the exchange rate, but costs were one-half those of the United States, then the food budget (i.e., the amount of food consumed) in the other country would be two-thirds that of the United States. If two countries are spending the same amount of money on Caesarean sections before differences in the cost of the operation are considered, but the cost of a Caesarean in one country is half that of the other, twice as many operations are being performed in the less expensive country.

Table 14. Health Expenditure per Capita, 2018 (or nearest year) (in US dollars expressed in purchasing power terms)

	Government/ Compulsory	Voluntary/ Out-of-Pocket	Total
United States	8,949	1,637	10,586
Germany	5,056	930	5,986
Australia[1]	3,467	1,538	5,005
Canada	3,466	1,508	4,974
France	4,141	824	4,965
Japan	4,008	758	4,766
United Kingdom	3,138	931	4,070
Italy	2,545	883	3,428

Note: Expenditure excludes investments.
[1]Australian expenditure estimates exclude all expenditure for residential aged care facilities in welfare (social) services.
Source: OECD (2019b).

Table 15. Health Expenditure as a Share of GDP, 2018 (or nearest year)

	Government/ Compulsory	Voluntary/ Out-of-Pocket	Total
United States	14.3	2.6	16.9
Germany	9.5	1.7	11.2
France	9.3	1.9	11.2
Japan	9.2	1.7	10.9
Canada	7.5	3.3	10.7
United Kingdom	7.5	2.2	9.8
Australia[1]	6.4	2.8	9.3
Italy	6.5	2.3	8.8

Note: Expenditure excludes investments.
[1]Australian expenditure estimates exclude all expenditure for residential aged care facilities in welfare (social) services.
Source: OECD (2019b).

With respect to another indicator of cost, OOP expenditure as a percentage of final consumption, the United States does not stand out in the same way, in part because total consumption is greater in the United States than elsewhere, although the across-country differences in absolute terms are not great (see **Table 16**).

Table 16. Out-of-Pocket Spending (as share of final household consumption, 2017 or latest year)

Italy	3.4
Australia	3.0
United States	2.8
Canada	2.8
Germany	2.7
Japan	2.6
United Kingdom	2.4
France	2.0

Source: OECD (2019b).

Table 17. Life Expectancy at Birth, 1970 and 2017 (or nearest year)

	1970	2017
Japan	72.0	84.2
Italy	72.0	83.0
Australia	70.8	82.6
France	72.2	82.6
Canada	72.9	82.0
United Kingdom	71.9	81.3
Germany	70.6	81.1
United States	70.9	78.6

Note: For Canada and Italy, the earlier year is 1971, not 1970.
Source: OECD (2019b).

Notwithstanding the large gap in per capita spending levels between the United States and the other seven countries, standard macro-indicators of quality make the United States look mediocre. Specifically, life expectancy at birth for a recent year puts the United States at the bottom rather than the top of the pack (see **Table 17**).

A sizable if less pronounced gap is observable for life expectancies at age 65 (see **Table 18**).

Part of the gap between the United States and the life-expectancy front-runners can be attributed—statistically at least—to mortality from preventable causes. Deaths related to lifestyle and treatable illnesses are highest in

Table 18. Life Expectancy in Years at Age 65, 1970 and 2017 (or nearest year)

	Women		Men		Total	
	1970	2017	1970	2017	1970	2017
Japan	15.3	24.4	12.5	19.6	13.9	22.0
France	16.8	23.6	13.0	19.6	14.9	21.6
Australia	15.6	22.3	11.9	19.7	13.8	21.0
Italy	16.2	22.4	13.3	19.2	14.8	20.8
Canada	17.5	22.1	13.7	19.3	15.6	20.7
United Kingdom	16.0	21.1	12.0	18.8	14.0	20.0
Germany	14.9	21.2	11.9	18.1	13.4	19.7
United States	17.0	20.6	13.1	18.1	15.1	19.4

Note: For Canada and Italy, the earlier year is 1971, not 1970.
Source: OECD (2019b).

the United States (OECD 2019b). For example, according to the OECD, death rates from opioids exceed those in the comparator countries by a wide margin, except for Canada (**Table 19**). The increased incidence of suicide and alcoholism also limits life expectancy in the same working-class white demographic group that is affected by opioids. See Case and Deaton (2017).[71] The way health care in the United States is financed means that quality of health care and treatment for preventable illnesses are more dependent on income in the US than they are in the other countries.

In any case, putting too much weight on aggregate indicators presents a problem. Life expectancy is shaped by many influences. Another way of judging the quality of health care is to look more directly at the apparent impact of health on the morbidity and mortality of specific diseases or conditions. This approach might allow us to zero in on the curative effects of health care regarding particular conditions, although it is obviously hard to derive an overall judgment from such a bottom-up approach. Nonetheless, depending on the condition, the relative performance of the United States improves. For example, five-year net survival rates from breast cancer in the United States compare favorably with the survival rates of the comparator countries (see **Table 20**). The comparison is less favorable for colon and rectal cancer, where they fall short of survival rates in Australia, Canada, and Japan (see **Table 21**).

[71]Case and Deaton (2020) note that these "deaths of despair" also have been on the rise in the other English-speaking industrial countries. They point to chronic wage stagnation as the cause, aggravated in the United States by that country's relatively ungenerous social safety net.

Table 19. Opioid-Related Deaths per Million Inhabitants, 2011–2016

	2011	2016
Italy	4.8	1.8
France	2.7	2.8
Germany		9.5
Australia	16.6	15.0
England & Wales	28.4	40.9
Canada		120.0
United States	73.8	131.0

Note: For Canada, the second year is 2018. No data are reported for Japan.
Source: OECD (2019b).

Table 20. Breast Cancer Five-Year Net Survival Rates, All Stages, 2010–2014 (in percent)

United States	90.2
Australia	89.5
Japan	89.4
Canada	88.6
Germany	86.0
Italy	86.0
United Kingdom	85.6

Note: Except for the United Kingdom, coverage is less than 100% of the national population. No data are reported for France.
Source: OECD (2019b).

As we have seen, the United States and some other countries, particularly Canada and the United Kingdom, do share some substantial similarities between the financing of the public and private components of pensions. The same cannot be said of the financing of either health care or LTC. The US health care system is distinct in its less-than-full coverage for residents who have not yet reached the age of 65 years, for the large role played by private insurance, and for the disparity in both the breadth and quality of coverage provided by private insurance—a feature sometimes referred to as tiering.

Table 21. Colon Cancer Five-Year Net Survival Rates, 2010–2014 (in percent)

Australia	70.7
Japan	67.8
Canada	67.0
United States	64.9
Germany	64.8
Italy	64.2
France	63.7
United Kingdom	60.0

Note: Except for Australia and the United Kingdom, rates represent less than full coverage of the national population.
Source: OECD (2019b).

As a result of the passage of the Affordable Care Act in 2010, the coverage of a core set of services in the United States reached an all-time high of 90.9% in 2015, according to the OECD (2017). The rate of coverage has fallen under the current administration. In the rest of the G–7 countries and in Australia, coverage is universal. The role of private insurers in the United States is the highest in the group—private primary insurance covered 55.3% of the population in 2015.

Age 65 is a watershed age for health care coverage in the United States. Coverage of Medicare Parts A and B is effectively universal, and the supplementary private plans cover about six-sevenths of the over-65 age-group (see Chapter 2). No such blanket coverage exists for older Americans who are not yet eligible for Medicare. These individuals likely will be covered by a policy provided by their employer—if their employer is midsize or large[72]—because employer-provided coverage is treated favorably by the tax code. Because coverage is employer based, however, it normally is lost if an employee loses or leaves the job, or soon afterward.[73]

This is not the case with any of the other countries. In the United States, even if someone has lost one job at a relatively late age and finds another

[72]In the United States, the Affordable Care Act requires employers with 50 or more employees to provide an employer-sponsored health insurance policy, with some exceptions. It does not require the employer to pay for the insurance, but most companies do pay a large fraction of the cost.

[73]A US provision in the Consolidated Omnibus Budget Reconciliation Act of 1985 (COBRA) allows terminated employees, and those who leave employment voluntarily, to continue health insurance for a certain period of time at their own expense.

job quickly, the new employer may not necessarily provide health insurance to its new employee. The obligation to do so applies only to midsize and large employers, and because of the various exceptions, an employee can fall through the cracks. The lack of insurance tied to employment can keep workers effectively trapped in jobs when they otherwise would be better off in another position at another place of work. The Affordable Care Act makes insurance available that is not connected to employment, but it often does so at a high price to the insured while offering limited coverage with high deductibles.

Finally, and in marked contrast to its position as leader of the pack in health expenditure, the United States is at the bottom in its expenditure on LTC as a percentage of GDP. This mainly reflects the comparative youthfulness of its population, especially in comparison with Europe and Japan (see **Table 22**).

Table 22. Long-Term Care Expenditure as a Percentage of GDP

	Health Component	Social Component	Total
Canada	1.3	...	1.3
France	1.3	0.6	1.9
Germany	1.5	0.0	1.5
Italy	0.7	...	0.7
Japan	1.8	...	1.8
United Kingdom	1.2	0.3	1.4
United States	0.6	...	0.6
Australia	0.2	...	0.2

Note: The health component relates to nursing and personal care, as well as palliative care and institutional and home care. The social component primarily covers help with the activities of daily living.
Source: OECD (2019b).

References

Abbott, Michael G., Charles M. Beach, Robin Boadway, and James C. MacKinnon. 2009. *Retirement Policy Issues in Canada*. McGill-Queen's University Press.

Aon Hewitt. 2012. The Real Deal—2012 Retirement Income Adequacy at Large Companies. Available at www.aon.com.

———. 2015. The Real Deal—Retirement Income Adequacy at Large Corporations. Available at www.aon.com.

———. 2018. The Real Deal—Retirement Income Adequacy Study. Available at www.aon.com.

Arnott, Robert D., Katrina Sherrerd, and Lillian Wu. 2013. "The Glidepath Illusion… and Potential Solutions." *Journal of Retirement* 1 (2): 13–28.

Australian Government. 2018. Productivity Commission. Superannuation: Assessing Efficiency and Competitiveness. Productivity Commission Inquiry Report. Overview (December).

———. 2020. Services Australia. Age Pension. Available at https://www.servicesaustralia.gov.au/individuals/services/centrelink/age-pension.

Banerjee, Sudipto. 2015. "Change in Household Spending after Retirement: Results from a Longitudinal Sample." *EBRI Issue Brief* 420 (November). Available at www.ebri.org.

Bee, Adam, and Joshua Mitchell. 2017. Do Older Americans Have More Income than We Think? SESHD Working Paper #2017-39 (July).

Biggs, Andrew G. 2017. "The Life Cycle Model, Replacement Rates and Retirement Income Adequacy." *Journal of Retirement* 4 (3): 96–110.

Biggs, Andrew G., and Sylvester Schieber. 2014. Responding to Teresa Ghilarducci on the Retirement Crisis. American Enterprise Institute (October 6).

Boivie, Ilana, and Nari Rhee. 2015. "The Continuing Retirement Saving Crisis." National Institute on Retirement Security (March). Available at www.nirs.org.

Brady, Peter J. 2007. *Optimal Savings: Would We Know It If We Saw It?* Unpublished.

———. 2010. "Measuring Retirement Income Adequacy." *Journal of Pension Economics and Finance* 9 (2): 235–62.

———. 2016. *How America Supports Retirement: Challenging the Conventional Wisdom on Who Benefits*. Washington, DC: Investment Company Institute.

Butrica, Barbara A., Joshua H. Goldwyn, and Richard W. Johnson. 2005. Understanding Expenditure Patterns in Retirement. Center for Retirement Research Working Paper 2005-03 (January).

Case, Anne, and Angus Deaton. 2017. "Mortality and Morbidity in the 21st Century." *Brookings Papers on Economic Activity* (Spring).

———. 2020. "The Epidemic of Despair: Will America's Mortality Crisis Spread to the Rest of the World?" *Foreign Affairs* 99 (2): 92–102.

Coe, N., and A. Webb. 2010. Children and Household Utility: Evidence from Kids Flying the Coop. Center for Retirement Research at Boston College Working Paper (2010–16). Available at www.crr.bc.edu.

Committee for a Responsible Federal Budget. 2019. Analysis of the 2019 Social Security Trustees' Report (April 22). Available at www.crfb.org/papers/analysis-2019-social-security-trustees-report.

Correia, Candice L., Richard Sayre, and Jessica C. Allen. 2017. "Avoiding the Medicaid Trap: A Step by Step Guide to Estate Planning." *Journal of Retirement* 4 (2): 96–103.

Crook, Michael, and Ronald Sutedja. 2017. "Will Long-Term Care Ruin Retirement Plans?" *Journal of Retirement* 4 (3): 63–76.

Davidson, Tom, and Keith Turner. 2015. "The Reverse Mortgage: A Strategic Lifetime Income Planning Resource." *Journal of Retirement* 3 (2): 61–79.

Dushi, Irena, Alicia Munnell, Geoffrey T. Sanzenbacher, and Anthony Webb. 2016. "Do Households Save More When the Kids Leave Home?" CRR Brief No. 16-8. Available at www.crr.bc.edu.

EBRI. 2019. 2019 Retirement Confidence Survey Summary Report (April 23). Available at https://www.ebri.org/docs/default-source/rcs/2019-rcs/2019-rcs-short-report.pdf?sfvrsn=85543f2f_4.

EBSA. 2016. Private Penson Plan Bulletin Historical Tables and Graphs 1975–2014 (September).

Fidelity. 2018. Four Rules of Thumb for Retirement (August 16). Available at Fidelity.com.

Genworth. 2016. 2016 Cost of Care Study (April).

Giordano, Shelley. 2015. *What's the Deal with Reverse Mortgages?* People Tested Media.

Gustman, Alan, Thomas Steinmeier, and Nahid Tabatabai. 2010. *Pensions in the Health and Retirement Study*. Harvard.

Hurd, Michael D., and Susann Rohwedder. 2008. The Retirement Consumption Puzzle: Actual Spending Change in Panel Data. NBER Working Paper No. 13929 (April).

———. 2011. Economic Preparation for Retirement. NBER Working Paper No. 17203 (July).

Ilmanen, Antti, Matthew Rauseo, and Liza Truax. 2016. "How Much Should DC Savers Worry about Expected Returns?" *Journal of Retirement* 4 (2): 44–53.

Kaiser Family Foundation. 2015. A Primer on Medicare—Key Facts about the Medicare Program and the People It Covers (March).

Knowledge@Wharton. (Jack Guttentag). 2015. Kosher Reverse Mortgages: Fixing a Dysfunctional Market (August).

Kolluri, Aurya, and Cynthia Hutchins. 2017. "Seven Life Priorities in Retirement." In *Financial Decision Making and Retirement Security in an Aging World*, ed. Olivia S. Mitchell, Brett Hammond, and Steven Utkus. Oxford University Press: 115–129.

Kotlikoff, Laurence. 2007. "Economics' Approach to Financial Planning."

Mackenzie, George A. (Sandy). 2006. *Annuity Markets and Pension Reform*. Cambridge University Press.

———. 2010. *The Decline of the Traditional Pension*. Cambridge University Press.

———. 2017. "Book Review: Finance for Normal People." *Journal of Retirement* 5 (1): 138–43.

———. 2019. "To Differ or Not To Differ (SPIA or DIA)." *Retirement Income Journal* (May 3).

Madamba, Anna, and Steven Utkus. 2017. Retirement Transitions in Four Countries. Vanguard Research (January). Available at https://institutional.vanguard.com.

Milevsky, Moshe A., and Huaxiong Huang. 2011. "Spending Retirement on Planet Vulcan: The Impact of Longevity Risk." *Financial Analysts Journal* 67 (2): 45–58.

Miller, Billie Jean, and Sylvester Schieber. 2014. "Contribution of Pension and Retirement Savings to Retirement Income Security: More Than Meets the Eye." *Journal of Retirement* 1 (3): 14–29.

Munnell, Alicia H., Anthony Webb, and Luke Delorme. 2006. Retirements at Risk: A New National Retirement Risk Index. Center for Retirement Research at Boston College. Available at www.crr.bc.edu.

Munnell, Alicia H., Anthony Webb, Francesca Golub Sass, and Dan Muldoon. 2009. Long-Term Care Costs and the National Retirement Risk Index. Center for Retirement Research at Boston College. No. 9–7 (March). Available at www.crr.bc.edu.

Munnell, Alicia H., Matthew S. Rutledge, and Anthony Webb, 2014–16. Are Retirees Falling Short? Reconciling the Conflicting Evidence. Center for Retirement Research at Boston College. Working Paper (November). Available at www.crr.bc.edu.

Munnell, Alicia H., Wenliang Hou, and Anthony Webb. 2015. "National Retirement Risk Index (NRRI) Update Shows Half of Working-Age Americans Still Falling Short." *Journal of Retirement* 3 (2): 34–42.

Munnell, Alicia H., and Anqi Chen. 2015. Do We Need a Price Index for the Elderly? Center for Retirement Research at Boston College. No. 15–18 (October). Available at www.crr.bc.edu.

Musumeci, Mary Beth, Priya Chidambaram, and Molly O'Malley Watts. 2019. Medicaid Financial Eligibility for Seniors and People with Disabilities: Findings from a 50-State Survey. Kaiser Foundation Issue Brief (June).

OASDI Trustees' 2019 Report. Short title for "The 2019 Annual Report of the Board of Trustees of the Federal Old-Age and Survivors Insurance and Federal Disability Insurance Funds."

OECD. 2017. Health at a Glance 2017. OECD and G20 Indicators.

———. 2018. Pensions Outlook 2018.

———. 2019a. Pensions at a Glance 2017. OECD and G20 Indicators.

———. 2019b. Health at a Glance 2017. OECD and G20 Indicators.

Pang, Gaobo, and Sylvester Schieber. 2014. "Why American Workers' Retirement Income Security Prospects Look So Bleak: A Review of Recent Assessments." *Journal of Retirement* 2 (1): 35–54.

Pang, Gaobo, and Mark Warshawsky. 2009. "Calculating Savings Rates in Working Years Needed to Maintain Living Standards in Retirement." *Benefits Quarterly* 25 (3): 31–42.

———. 2014. "Retirement Savings Adequacy of U.S. Workers." *Benefits Quarterly* 30 (First quarter): 29–38.

Rappaport, Anna M. 2018. "What are Retirees Doing and Saying?" *Benefits Quarterly* (Fourth quarter).

Rhee, Nari. 2013. "The Retirement Savings Crisis: Is It Worse than We Think?" National Institute on Retirement Security (June). Available at www.nirs.org.

Rudd, Andrew, and Laurence B. Siegel. 2013. "Using an Economic Balance Sheet for Financial Planning." *Journal of Wealth Management* 16 (2): 15–23.

Schieber, Sylvester. 2015. "U.S. Retirement Policy Considerations for the 21st Century." *Journal of Retirement* 3 (2): 12–33.

Scholz, John Karl, Ananth Seshadri, and Surachai Khitatrakun. 2006. "Are Americans Saving "Optimally" for Retirement?" *Journal of Political Economy* 114 (4): 607–643.

Scholz, J.K., and A. Seshadri. 2009. *Children and Household Wealth. Mimeo.* University of Wisconsin.

Sexauer, Stephen C., and Laurence B. Siegel. 2013. "A Pension Promise to Oneself." *Financial Analysts Journal* 69 (6): 13–32.

Simon, Ruth. 2018. "Booming Job Market Can't Quite Fill Retirement Shortfall." *Wall Street Journal* (December 21).

Social Security Administration. 2019. Annual Reports. Available at www.ssa.gov/OACT/TRSUM/index.html.

Society of Actuaries. 2017. 2017 Risks and Process of Retirement Survey: Report of Findings. Available at www.soa.org.

Statman, Meir. 2017. *Finance for Normal People*. New York City: Oxford University Press.

Transamerica Center for Retirement Studies. 2016. The Current State of Retirement: A Compendium of Findings about American Retirees (April).

Turner, John A. 2017. "Social Security Policy Procrastination: A Behavioral Economics Perspective." *Journal of Retirement* 5 (1): 32–47.

VanDerhei, Jack. 2014a. "What Causes EBRI Retirement Readiness Ratings™ to Vary: Results from the 2014 Retirement Security Projection Model®." *EBRI Issue Brief* 396 (February). Available at www.ebri.org.

———. 2014b. "Short" Falls: Who's Most Likely to Come Up Short in Retirement, and When? *EBRI Notes* 35 (6). Available at www.ebri.org.

———. 2018. *EBRI Retirement Security Projection Model.* RSPM. Power point presentation.

VanDerhei, Jack, and Craig Copeland. 2010. "The EBRI Retirement Readiness Rating:™ Retirement Income Preparation and Future Prospects." *EBRI Issue Brief* 344 (July). Available at www.ebri.org.

Warshawsky, Mark. 2017. "Retire on the House? The Doubtful Use of Reverse Mortgages to Enhance Retirement Security." *Journal of Retirement* 5 (3): 10–31.

Warshawsky, Mark J., and Ross A. Marchand. 2017. "Improving the System of Financing Long-Term Services and Supports for Older Americans." *Journal of Retirement* 5 (1): 48–68.

The CFA Institute Research Foundation Board of Trustees 2019–2020

Officers and Directors

Research Foundation Review Board

Named Endowments

The CFA Institute Research Foundation acknowledges with sincere gratitude the generous contributions of the Named Endowment participants listed below.

Gifts of at least US$100,000 qualify donors for membership in the Named Endowment category, which recognizes in perpetuity the commitment toward unbiased, practitioner-oriented, relevant research that these firms and individuals have expressed through their generous support of the CFA Institute Research Foundation.

Ameritech
Anonymous
Robert D. Arnott
Theodore R. Aronson, CFA
Asahi Mutual Life Insurance Company
Batterymarch Financial Management
Boston Company
Boston Partners Asset Management, L.P.
Gary P. Brinson, CFA
Brinson Partners, Inc.
Capital Group International, Inc.
Concord Capital Management
Dai-Ichi Life Insurance Company
Daiwa Securities
Mr. and Mrs. Jeffrey Diermeier
Gifford Fong Associates
Investment Counsel Association of America, Inc.
Jacobs Levy Equity Management
John A. Gunn, CFA
John B. Neff, CFA
Jon L. Hagler Foundation
Long-Term Credit Bank of Japan, Ltd.
Lynch, Jones & Ryan, LLC
Meiji Mutual Life Insurance Company
Miller Anderson & Sherrerd, LLP
Nikko Securities Co., Ltd.
Nippon Life Insurance Company of Japan
Nomura Securities Co., Ltd.
Payden & Rygel
Provident National Bank
Frank K. Reilly, CFA
Salomon Brothers
Sassoon Holdings Pte. Ltd.
Scudder Stevens & Clark
Security Analysts Association of Japan
Shaw Data Securities, Inc.
Sit Investment Associates, Inc.
Standish, Ayer & Wood, Inc.
State Farm Insurance Company
Sumitomo Life America, Inc.
T. Rowe Price Associates, Inc.
Templeton Investment Counsel Inc.
Frank Trainer, CFA
Travelers Insurance Co.
USF&G Companies
Yamaichi Securities Co., Ltd.

Senior Research Fellows

Financial Services Analyst Association